T0224604

# Lecture Notes in Computer Science     8594

*Commenced Publication in 1973*
Founding and Former Series Editors:
Gerhard Goos, Juris Hartmanis, and Jan van Leeuwen

More information about this series at http://www.springer.com/series/7409

Michael Behrisch · Daniel Krajzewicz
Melanie Weber (Eds.)

# Simulation of Urban Mobility

First International Conference, SUMO 2013
Berlin, Germany, May 15–17, 2013
Revised Selected Papers

 Springer

*Editors*
Michael Behrisch
Daniel Krajzewicz
Melanie Weber
Institute of Transportation Systems
German Aerospace Center
Berlin
Germany

ISSN 0302-9743          ISSN 1611-3349   (electronic)
ISBN 978-3-662-45078-9      ISBN 978-3-662-45079-6   (eBook)
DOI 10.1007/978-3-662-45079-6

Library of Congress Control Number: 2014954578

Springer Heidelberg New York Dordrecht London

Springer is part of Springer Science+Business Media (www.springer.com)

# Preface

The simulation of road traffic and especially individual vehicular mobility in larger conurbations presents a number of challenges in various areas of research such as physics, engineering, and computer science as well as psychology and sociology. The search for an appropriate and practically usable model for the problems of mode choice, route choice as well as the behavior of drivers when following each other, changing lanes or reacting to junction priorities and traffic lights created a number of complex software packages. Together with the advance of vehicular communication systems the requirements to those simulations and especially to their interfaces increased significantly. This lead to a wider use of open source packages such as the Simulation of Urban Mobility (SUMO) suite developed mainly at the Institute of Transportation Systems of the German Aerospace Center.

This volume contains the proceedings of the First SUMO User Conference (SUMO 2013), which was held during May 15–17, 2013 in Berlin-Adlershof, Germany. SUMO is a well-established microscopic traffic simulation suite which has been available since 2001 and provides a wide range of traffic planning and simulation tools. The conference proceedings give a good overview of the applicability and usefulness of simulation tools like SUMO ranging from new methods in traffic control and vehicular communication to the simulation of complete cities. Another aspect of the tool suite, its universal extensibility due to the availability of the source code, is reflected in contributions covering parallelization and workflow improvements to govern microscopic traffic simulation results.

Several articles give short outlines of the general workflow when setting up a simulation with SUMO as well as an overview about the available tools for net and demand generation and for the evaluation of the results. Further features include the simulation of private and public transport modes, person-based trip chains as well as the extension for the implementation of new behavioral models or remote control of the simulation using various programing environments. The conference's aim was bringing together the large international user community and exchanging experience in using SUMO, while presenting results or solutions obtained using the software. This collection should inspire you to try your next project with the SUMO suite as well or to find new applications in your existing environment.

July 2014

Michael Behrisch
Daniel Krajzewicz
Melanie Weber

# SUMO 2013 Organization

SUMO 2013 was organized by the Institute of Transportation Systems, German Aerospace Center, Berlin.

## International Scientific Committee

| | |
|---|---|
| Ana L.C. Bazzan | Universidade Federal do Rio Grande do Sul, Brazil |
| Robbin Blokpoel | Imtech Traffic & Infra, The Netherlands |
| David Eckhoff | University of Erlangen, Germany |
| Jérôme Härri | Institute EURECOM, France |
| Daniel Krajzewicz | German Aerospace Center, Germany |
| Mario Krumnow | University of Technology Dresden, Germany |
| Michaela Milano | DEIS Università di Bologna, Italy |
| Andreas Schadschneider | University of Cologne, Germany |
| Peter Wagner | German Aerospace Center, Germany |

## Organization Committee

| | |
|---|---|
| Michael Behrisch | German Aerospace Center, Germany |
| Daniel Krajzewicz | German Aerospace Center, Germany |
| Melanie Weber | German Aerospace Center, Germany |

# Contents

# Models and Technical Innovations

# SUMO's Road Intersection Model

Jakob Erdmann$^{(\boxtimes)}$ and Daniel Krajzewicz

Institute of Transportation Systems, German Aerospace Center, Berlin, Germany
{jakob.erdmann,daniel.krajzewicz}@dlr.de

**Abstract.** Besides basic models for longitudinal and lateral movement, a traffic simulation needs also models and algorithms for right-of-way rules. This publication describes how passing an intersection is modeled within SUMO, including a description of an earlier and the currently used model.

**Keywords:** Road traffic simulation · Intersection model

## 1 Introduction

SUMO [1, 2] is an open source road traffic simulation package developed at the Institute of Transportation Systems at the German Aerospace Center. SUMO is a microscopic traffic simulation which means that each vehicle is modeled explicitly. Independently configurable models are used to define different aspects of each vehicle's driving dynamics. Multiple car-following models which describe longitudinal movements are implemented as well as multiple lane-changing models that realize lateral movements. The models used in SUMO were initially described in [3]. For simulation of real-life networks, further models are necessary. This paper describes the current implementation of the intersection control model used in SUMO. An earlier less detailed model which was tied to a fixed simulation time step length of 1 s is also described. The current model was implemented in order to overcome this earlier model's limitations.

This documented presents an extension to the description of the intersection model given in [4]. It describes new features such as the modeling of stop signs and the intersection type all-way stop. Additionally, the revised dynamics in regard to link leaders is described. The topics of driver impatience and blocked intersections are further additions to the preceding work.

The rest of this document is structured as following: In Sect. 2, the original and the currently used model for intersection control are described. One aspect of the intersection model is the estimation of time windows in which a vehicle will occupy the intersection. The accuracy of this estimation is the subject of the Sect. 3. In Sect. 4 we present our conclusions.

## 2 Intersection Model

Generally, road networks are represented as graphs in SUMO. An intersection ("node") consists of incoming and outgoing edges. An "edge" represents a unidirectional road

© Springer-Verlag Berlin Heidelberg 2014
M. Behrisch et al. (Eds.): SUMO 2013, LNCS 8594, pp. 3–17, 2014.
DOI: 10.1007/978-3-662-45079-6_1

with one or more lanes. Each lane has a unique id which is derived from the edge id and the numerical index of the lane starting with 0 at the rightmost lane. The lanes of incoming edges are called incoming lanes and the lanes of outgoing edges are called outgoing lanes. Within an intersection lie so called "internal lanes" which connect the incoming lanes with the outgoing lanes. Vehicle movements across an intersection proceed along these internal lanes just as they would on regular lanes. Internal lanes were added to the simulation to obtain fine grained vehicle trajectories and to better model the capacity of intersections.

A given lane may have more than one successor lanes. The connectivity among lanes is defined with "links". This gives rise to the "lane-graph" where lanes are connected by links in contrast to the "intersection-graph" where intersections are connected with roads.

In older versions of SUMO, before the introduction of internal lanes, there was a link between an incoming lane and an outgoing lane. Vehicles have seemingly "jumped" across an intersection. Since the introduction of internal lanes there is a link between an incoming lane and an internal lane (called an "entry link" and another link between the internal lane and an outgoing lane (called an "exit link") as shown in Fig. 1. The entry links of an intersection are numbered from 0 to n. Since there is exactly one exit link for each entry link, the link index uniquely defines a connection across the intersection from an incoming lane to an outgoing lane. The link indices are computed using the following scheme: first, the incoming edges are sorted in clockwise fashion. Then, the lanes, starting at the top-most are traversed. The links outgoing from a lane are then iterated, starting with the right-most destination, relative to the incoming edge. These link indices are used to uniquely identify a connection when specifying right of way rules.

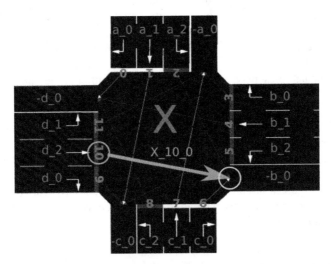

**Fig. 1.** Intersection model terminology in SUMO. The intersection has id X and features the incoming roads a, b, c, d and the outgoing edges, −a, −b, −c, −d. The connection from incoming lane d_2 to outgoing lane −b_0 crosses X on the internal lane X_10_0. The entry link with index 10 is circled at the left. The exit link is circled at the right.

At most intersections, vehicles wait at the stop line at the border of the intersection until they may cross conflicting streams of traffic. However, on some types of inter-sections, left-turning vehicles are allowed to wait in the middle of the intersection. This is modelled in SUMO by splitting internal lanes at the halting position and introducing an "internal intersection" that lies within the original intersection. Vehicles using these internal lanes always pass the entry link to the intersection and then wait at the internal intersection instead. The right-of-way computation for internal intersections follows the same principles as that of regular intersections.

## 2.1   Earlier Model

The right-of-way model that was implemented in the initial releases of SUMO is a strong simplification of real world behavior. When approaching an intersection a vehicle at first sets the information about its approach to the intersection. After this has been done for all vehicles, the intersection "decides" which vehicles are allowed to pass without braking and which vehicles have to yield. This is done using a right-of-way matrix. This matrix describes which connections cross each other and which one has the right of way in case of crossing connections. This concept is illustrated in the following using an example.

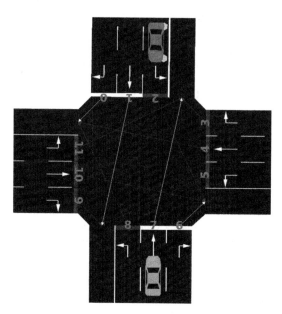

**Fig. 2.** Two vehicles (top and bottom) are approaching intersection X from Fig. 1. The top vehicle has to yield to the vehicle oncoming from the bottom on link 7 before it can make a left turn on link 2 (Color figure online).

Figure 2 shows an intersection which is approached from the top by a vehicle on link 2 and from the bottom by a vehicle on link 7. Since the paths of both vehicles intersect and both wish to cross the intersection in overlapping time intervals, a right of way computation is performed. In Fig. 3 the right-of-way matrix for this intersection is shown, emphasizing links 2 and 7. The matrix cell with row i and column j defines the right of way for a vehicle approaching link $i$ (called the "ego"-vehicle) in regards to another vehicle approaching link $j$ (called the "other"-vehicle). Depending on the colors white, yellow or red, the ego vehicle ignores, has priority over or yields to the other vehicle. In the example, the top vehicle (link 2) yields to the bottom vehicle (link 7) because of the red box in cell (2, 7) which agrees with the common rules of traffic for left-turning vehicles. This is mirrored by the yellow cell (7, 2) which indicates that the bottom vehicle has priority over the top vehicle.

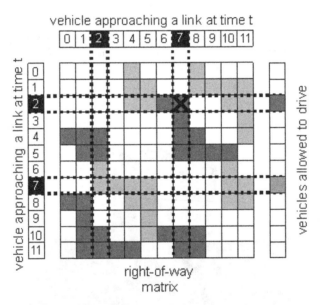

**Fig. 3.** The right-of-way matrix of the intersection shown in Fig. 2. Row i corresponds to the crossing/priority relation for link i. Link 7 crosses links 2, 3, 4, 5, 10, 11 but has the right of way (yellow/light grey boxes). Link 2 crosses links 4, 5, 6, 7, 10, 11 but must yield to 6 and 7 as indicated by red (dark grey) boxes. Since a vehicle approaches on link 7 (in the relevant time interval) the vehicle on link 2 has to brake (Color figure online).

The matrix itself is static and computed during the network import/generation. In the initial intersection model, traffic lights were implemented by removing the information about vehicles approaching links with a red signal. As the participation in determining which vehicles may drive is invalidated for these links by doing so, these vehicles are not allowed to pass the intersection and also do not hinder vehicles at other links.

Even though this model works well for simulation steps of one second, it caused problems when implementing sub-second time steps. Because the decision about letting a vehicle pass the intersection is performed in each time step, vehicles must not drive faster than their maximum braking ability multiplied with the step size time when being in front of the intersection. This is necessary to ensure that the vehicle can still brake if another vehicle with higher priority suddenly approaches. When decreasing the duration of simulation steps, this velocity is decreasing by the same factor, too, as depicted in Fig. 4.

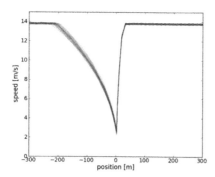 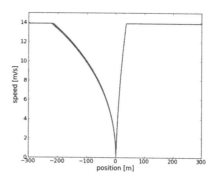

**Fig. 4.** Vehicle speed when approaching an intersection in the old model; (a) simulation steps of 1 s, (b) simulation steps of 0.1 s.

This wrong behavior for lower step times was the motivation to change the intersection control algorithm. Another important motivation was the need to model the interaction between vehicles which occupy the intersection simultaneously. This became necessary after the introduction of internal lanes on which vehicles may decelerate or even stop. This requires other vehicles to react in order to avoid collisions.

From an architectural standpoint, transferring the logic for passing an intersection from the intersection model into the driver model is assumed to be a development step into the right direction, allowing further work on driver behavior modeling.

## 2.2    Requirements for an Improved Model

The goal for an improved intersection control model was to support all types of intersection typically found around the world and to allow for realistic simulation dynamics. The following intersection types are deemed necessary:

- Intersections without prioritization
  - right-before-left
  - all-way stop.
- Prioritized intersections with
  - Different directions of the prioritized road (straight, turning),
  - Unprioritized roads with yield or stop signs.
- Intersections controlled by traffic lights.

Important aspects of realistic intersection dynamics are the following:

- No deadlocks,
- No collisions,
- Efficient use of the intersection,
- Realistic acceptance gaps,
- Approaching unprioritized links without stopping,
- Qualitative dynamics independent of the simulation step length.

The current intersection model meets all these goals.

## 2.3   Current Model

In this section we describe features which distinguish the current intersection model from the previous intersection model. These features were implemented over a time frame of more than 10 years following a growing list of requirements. The complete specification of all implemented formulas and decision trees cannot be given due to lack of space. However, the described concepts should serve as a useful guide when reading the implementation sources of SUMO [5].

**Approaching an Intersection.** The key to correct the deficiencies of the original model described in Sect. 2.1 was to not only consider the current time step, but to give the right of way based on information about oncoming vehicles including an extrapolation of their time of arrival at the intersection. To do so, each vehicle informs the entry link about its approach. In contrary to the initial model, not only the approach as such is stored, but also the expected time of arrival at the intersection and the speed at arrival. Using this information, the time within which a certain vehicle will occupy the intersection can be computed. Each entry link also stores information about its "foe links". This corresponds to the red boxes in one row of the right-of-way matrix shown in Fig. 3. When approaching an intersection (an entry link), a vehicle computes how long it will occupy the intersection and then checks against all approaching vehicles in all foe links of its entry link. If the requested time slot is separated from all approaching foe time slots by a suitable safety gap the vehicle is allowed to pass the entry link and thus enter the intersection. When the ego vehicle and the approaching foe vehicle have the same target lane, safety depends on the speed difference between both vehicles. The formula which determines whether a given situation is safe uses the same idea as that used in car following, namely that the follower vehicle $F$ with velocity $v_F$ and deceleration $d_F$ needs to be able to stop before the leader vehicle $L$ (with velocity $v_L$ and deceleration $d_L$) does:

$$v_L^2/d_L > v_F^2/d_F \qquad (1)$$

A vehicle informs the entry links to the next few intersections on its current route (up to a distance of about 3000 m) about its approach. Due to the advance knowledge of approaching foe vehicles, a vehicle approaching on an unprioritized link cannot be "surprised" by the sudden appearance of a foe. This allows decoupling the approach speed from the simulation step size. Instead, vehicles decelerate up to a fixed distance from the stopping line (default 4.5 m, corresponding to the default vehicle deceleration of 4.5 m/s$^2$). If braking is not necessary at this point they can safely accelerate and cross the intersection. Otherwise they stop until there is a suitable gap in traffic.

Figure 5 shows that using this implementation assures similar behavior for different simulation step sizes. The velocity used for approaching the intersection is the vehicle's deceleration capability multiplied with 1 s. For the standard Krauß parameters it is equal to 16.2 km/h, what was found to be empirically valid when compared to measures obtained from test drives with DLR test vehicles. Within the current model, the vehicle's maximum deceleration ability is used for all intersections and all directions of driving across them. Because in reality, this speed is mainly dictated by the possibility to look into foe lanes for determining whether the intersection may be crossed, further extensions of the model, in means of differing between approach velocities promise to improve the model's quality. It should be also noted that the simulated time line of deceleration and acceleration is not yet matching the reality.

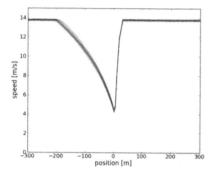 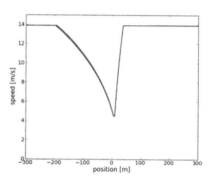

**Fig. 5.** Vehicle speed when approaching an intersection in the new model. (a) simulation steps of 1 s, (b) simulation steps of 0.1 s.

**Dynamics within an Intersection.** Once a vehicle enters an intersection by passing the entry link, this link is no longer informed. Since vehicles follow normal movement rules while on the intersection they may brake while on the intersection or even come to a stop. Therefore, other vehicles require an additional mechanism for keeping track of vehicles currently on the intersection in order to avoid collisions. The new implementation is designed to re-use the existing functionality of the car-following model for letting vehicles maintain safe distances while interacting within the intersection. Normally, this functionality is only active for vehicles which move on identical or subsequent lanes. At an intersection however, vehicles are on different lanes which cross somewhere on the intersection or merge into the same outgoing lane.

To be able to use the car following functions two things are required.

1. A vehicle needs to know the lead vehicle;
2. There must be a well-defined distance between the follower and the lead vehicle.

The first point is accomplished by declaring the first vehicle of any two vehicles to enter the intersection as the leader. This is particularly important, because several vehicles may be driving within the space of the intersection at the same time and there must be a non-circular leader-follow relation among them to avoid deadlocks (technically speaking, all vehicles must be in an antisymmetric, transitive and irreflexive relation). The second point is accomplished by virtually superimposing both internal lanes up to the crossing point. If both internal lanes merge into the same outgoing lane, the crossing point is naturally the beginning of the outgoing lane.

We describe the position of the crossing point relative to the start of the respective internal lanes. Let $A$ denote the lane on which the leader vehicle drives and let $B$ denote the lane on which the follower vehicle drives. The position of the crossing point of $A$ and $B$ on lane $A$, $pos(C_{AB})$ is the driving distance from the start of lane $A$ to the geometrical crossing point (disregarding the width of the lanes). Likewise, $pos(C_{BA})$ is the position of the crossing point on lane $B$. Furthermore, $pos(L)$ is the position of the front of the leader vehicle $L$ relative to the start of $A$ and $pos(F)$ is the position of the follower vehicle $F$ relative to the start of $B$. We define the distance of $L$ from the crossing point $d_L$ and the distance of $F$ from the crossing point $d_F$

$$d_L := pos(C_{AB}) - pos(L) \tag{2}$$

$$d_F := pos(C_{BA}) - pos(F) \tag{3}$$

The distances $d_L$ and $d_F$ are visualized in Fig. 6. Using this notation, the virtual gap g between both vehicles is defined as

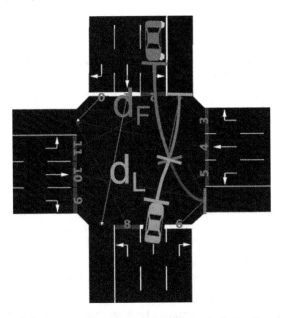

**Fig. 6.** Distance $d_L$ of the leader vehicle (approaching from the bottom) and $d_R$ of the follower vehicle (approaching from the top) to the crossing point of their future trajectories.

$$g := d_F - d_L - length(L) - minGap(F) \tag{4}$$

Where *length(L)* is the physical length of vehicle $L$ and *minGap(F)* is the minimum gap that vehicle $F$ intends to keep to its leader at all times. Note that $g$ may be negative which causes vehicle $F$ to stop.

In the current implementation each exit link maintains a list of "foe internal lanes". These are the lanes which correspond to the yellow and red boxes in one row of the right-of-way matrix in Fig. 3. In other words, these are the internal lanes which intersect with the internal lane the approaching vehicle intends to use.

A vehicle that wishes to pass an exit link on its route asks this link for any additional vehicles to which it must adapt its speed. These vehicles are called link leaders. The link checks all of its foe internal lanes for occupancy computes the virtual gap and returns each found vehicle as a potential link leader to be followed.

Figure 7 shows the same intersection as Fig. 1 with three vehicles A (driving from the bottom towards the top, B (following A on the same route) and C (driving from the left to the top). Vehicle C wishes to pass the exit link that belongs to link 11. Both vehicles A and B are on the same internal lane which is a foe internal lane for link 11. On the left side of Fig. 7, vehicles A and B are potential link leader for C. Since A and B have entered the intersection before C, they will both be followed. In this case only the speed adaption to B is relevant since B is already following A. On the right side of Fig. 7 the situation is slightly different. Vehicle C has already entered the intersection before vehicle B and therefore, C only follows A.

In the current implementation each vehicle maintains a list of link leaders being followed for each exit link. This list is used when maintaining the antisymmetric link leader relation among vehicles (vehicle C only sets vehicle B as its link leader if B does not already have C as its link leader).

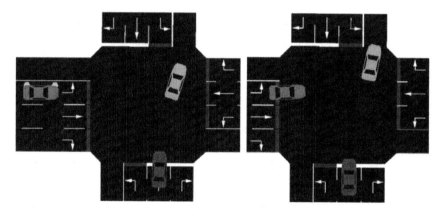

**Fig. 7.** Examples of link leader relations for the vehicles A (center), B (bottom) and C (left). In the left figure A is the leader of B and both are the leaders of C. In the right figure A is the leader of C and C is the leader of B because C entered the intersection before B.

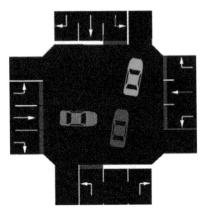

**Fig. 8.** The vehicle on the left wish to go straight may drive up to the point where its trajectory intersects with those of the other vehicles driving from bottom to top.

The use of the car-following model gives appropriate results if the vehicles $L$ and $F$ approach the same outgoing lane. However, if the vehicles approach different outgoing lanes and their trajectories cross somewhere on the intersection, the car-following model only returns an upper bound on the collision-free speed. This can be easily understood when considering the situation shown in Fig. 8. Here the vehicle on the left (C) is on a west-east trajectory across the intersection If the other vehicles (A, B) are stopped on the intersection, C may drive up to the crossing point without causing a collision even though the virtual gap $g$ may be negative (the lengths of A and B which influence $g$ are irrelevant here). To reflect this situation, the implementation lets vehicles drive with a speed that is as least as high as the maximum safe speed for stopping at the point where the trajectories cross. The computation of that speed is again left to the car-following model.

The link based model of detecting conflicting approach information coupled with the handling of link leaders allows for full vehicle dynamics on the intersection together with efficient use of the intersection as a natural extension of car following.

**Additional Intersection Types.** Another recent extension to the intersection model of SUMO was the ability to model additional intersection types. Intersections of the type "priority_stop" follow the same right of way rules as prioritized intersections but they require vehicles on minor roads to come to a complete stop before passing the intersection. This is accomplished by checking the "waitingTime" of the respective vehicle and forcing it to slow down unless that value is positive. As a consequence, vehicles may only pass the intersection after stopping briefly. The waitingTime of vehicles is among common vehicle attributes that are always tracked. It is incremented every simulation step if the vehicle's speed is equal or below a fixed threshold of 0.1 m/s and reset to 0 every time the vehicle's speed is above that threshold.

Intersections of type "allway_stop" also force the vehicles to slow down unless they have a positive waitingTime. Additionally, the waitingTime of each vehicle is recorded as part of the approach information. The right of way between two conflicting vehicles is given to that vehicle which has a higher waitingTime. This forces vehicles to stop briefly and pass the intersection in the order of their arrival.

**Impatience.** In the previous section it was described that the ego vehicle enters an intersection if its expected time frame of intersection occupancy is sufficiently distinct from the usage frames of all foe vehicles with higher priority. This is necessary to ensure a collision free intersection model. However, there is yet another degree of freedom which must be considered in this decision. Just as in reality, the ego vehicle may enter the intersection "aggressively", forcing foe vehicles to brake hard to maintain safety relations. Or it may refrain from entering the intersection until it can do so without disturbing other vehicles at all. Between these extremes lies a continuum of behaviours which all satisfy the requirements of a safe intersection model. We model this continuum using the term 'impatience' which is a real value from the interval [0, 1]. Vehicles with an impatience of 0 avoid actions which require other vehicles to slow down while vehicles with impatience 1 will enter an intersection even if other vehicles need to employ maximum deceleration to ensure safe driving distance. Generally speaking, a vehicle with impatience $\alpha$ will enter an intersection if it expects to leave it a time $t$ and

$$t < (1 - \alpha) \times a_{min} + \alpha \times a_{max} \qquad (5)$$

where $a_{min}$ is the earliest time of the foe vehicles arrival at the intersection and $a_{max}$ is the latest time of the foe vehicles arrival (using maximum deceleration). If the foe vehicle can come to a full stop before the intersection $a_{max}$ is set to a constant value of $C$ seconds to prevent $\alpha$ from becoming meaningless by having infinities in the equation. The current model uses $C = 30$ because it was found to work well but it was not put against real-world measures.

The choice of $\alpha$ for the simulation has important implications for the fluidity of traffic. If the value of $\alpha$ is too low, vehicles on an unprioritized road may be blocked from driving indefinitely while there is heavy traffic on the main road. If the value of $\alpha$ is near 1 traffic on the main road will be frequently disturbed in a manner that does not fit real world experience.

To avoid these problems, the value of $\alpha$ is dynamic in the simulation. The very name 'impatience' has been chosen because it implies something that grows over time. In the simulation the value of $\alpha$ is defined dynamically as:

$$\alpha := MAX(0, MIN(1, \alpha_C + waitingTime/T)) \qquad (6)$$

where $\alpha_C$ is a vehicle type specific constant defaulting to 0 which can be configured in the range $[-1, 1]$ to model the base level of driver impatience. The extreme values of $\alpha_C$ result in constant values for $\alpha$ of 0 and 1 respectively. The value of T is a configurable simulation constant which governs the time after which stopped vehicles will be removed to clear deadlocks (defaulting to 300 s). The value of T can be taken to model that maximum waiting time that vehicles will typically tolerate. If this time is exceeded the model is in an erroneous state (typically because a deadlock has developed) and this state is cleared by removing vehicles and inserting them at a later point on their route. Using this definition of $\alpha$, impatience of a vehicle (or rather its driver) grows while it is waiting to pass a link. This avoids major disturbances of traffic on the main road in most cases but allows some disturbance where necessary to avoid completely blocking the unprioritized road.

**Avoiding Blocked Intersections.** According to traffic laws [6, 7] it is forbidden to enter an intersection if there is a danger of not being able to pass the intersection and consequently blocking cross traffic. As this rule requires some judgement about the probable behaviour of downstream traffic and compliance to traffic laws is not perfect, blocked intersections do still occur in reality.

With the introduction of internal lanes to the intersection model of SUMO, the issue of blocked intersections must be addressed in the simulation as well. For every vehicle approaching an intersection, there is a check whether the vehicle will be able to leave the intersection and thus may begin entering the intersection. If this check fails the vehicle stops before the intersection and repeats the check every simulation step. As a side effect of a failed check, the stopping vehicle no longer prevents vehicles with lower priority from crossing its path. This is important because otherwise a jam on the priority road would immediately extend to any roads that cross it.

Just as in reality it is not a trivial thing to decide in advance whether a given vehicle will be able to leave the intersection. In the following we describe the heuristic that is used to prevent vehicles from blocking an intersection. The ego vehicle has a certain space requirement $s$ which consists of its physical length and the minimum standing gap to its predecessor vehicle, which must be met behind the intersection. The length of a vehicle and the size of the minimum gap are configurable attributes of a vehicle. The minimum gap is the distance which a vehicle must keep to its predecessor when both vehicles are stopped. If there is a stopped vehicle behind the intersection which leaves less than $s$ meters of space behind the intersection the check immediately fails. This idea is extended to cover cases where the leader vehicle is still moving.

For every simulation step there is a look-ahead horizon which the ego vehicles uses to plan future movements (mainly in regard to maintaining safe velocities and to follow its route). As a result of this horizon it is known which lanes the ego vehicle will drive on in the next simulation steps unless a lateral change of lanes occurs. Along these lanes a check is done until the first stopped vehicle is found or the lanes are exhausted. Along the way, the available space (lengths of the regular lanes) is accumulated as well as the space requirements of moving vehicles (length and minimum standing gap). The check succeeds only if the available space is sufficient to meet the combined space requirements of the ego vehicle and the moving vehicles up to the next stopped vehicle or the end of the look-ahead horizon. During the forward search along the future lanes of the ego vehicle two more things are treated just like stopped vehicles: closed links and vehicles which are about to stop. A closed link is one that prevents vehicle movements such as a red light or a minor road with incoming priority traffic. Whether a vehicle is about to stop is determined by checking that vehicle's tail lights and by checking whether the vehicle was flagged as about to stop in the previous simulation step. These flags are a technical solution for improving a driver's ability to anticipate the behavior of fellow drivers and can be thought of as modeling a driver's situational awareness.

It should be noted that the check by the ego vehicle is performed for all intersections along the look-ahead horizon. It may well be possible that the ego vehicle can safely enter the first intersection but has to slow down already because it may not enter the intersection after that. Another thing that must be considered is a minimum length for the look-ahead horizon. For reasons of avoiding collisions a vehicle only needs to look ahead as far as its current braking distance. However, to detect whether there is enough space ahead for leaving an intersection a larger look-ahead is sometimes needed. The current simulation model sets the minimum look-ahead distance to 5 times the length of the vehicle because this was found to work empirically. Taken together, these heuristics prevents blocked intersections in most situations. The few remaining failure cases are characterized by the emergence of jam conditions immediately after a successful check.

## 3   Estimation of Link Entry/Exit Times

In the following, the estimation of times and speeds of arrival and leaving an intersection is discussed. Figure 9 shows the deviations of the estimated speeds and times over time for a major (high prioritized) link. These vehicles do not have to break. "deviation" denotes here the difference value obtained by subtracting the real from the estimated value in the following Figures. One may see that the times of arrival and leaving are both estimated too low and only increasingly move towards the correct value. This is due to the random "dawdling" behavior of SUMO's default car-following model, see [8]. If the dawdling is disabled, the estimation is correct from the very begin on (not shown, here). The deviations in time are due to the same reason. They are straight, as in each time step, the estimation is based on the perfect speed (50 km/h in the shown example) and the dawdling is performed by the model afterwards. It should be noted, that the estimation could be more correct, if the dawdling, regarding its stochastic nature, would be taken into account during the computation of the times/speeds.

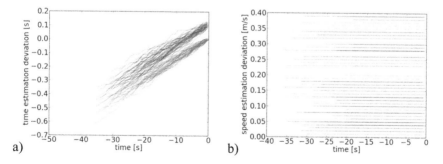

**Fig. 9.** Deviations of the estimated time (left) and speeds (right) from their final counterpart for arrival at an intersection (red) and leaving an intersection (blue) for vehicles which have the right of way. In the left figure, the blue curves are grouped at the top while the red curves are grouped at the bottom. In the right figure, red and blue curves are intermixed evenly (Color figure online).

The additional error in estimating the leave time is probably due to taking into account the distance to the leader in jam/when standing (SUMO's "minGap" attribute of a vehicle type), which was set to 2 m in the shown example; 2 m divided by 13.89 m/s gives the offset shown here, which is about 0.14 s.

The difference in starting times is due to using a random position for the place the vehicle departs at. This was done for adding randomness into the possible co–occurrences of vehicles at high and at low prioritized roads. The behavior of vehicles on prioritized roads is straightforward and can be easily explained, see above. But the behavior of vehicles that have to react to crossing traffic is more complicated. Shown in Fig. 10 the shape of time estimation development has three peculiarities. The first are large overestimations of the arrival and the leave time by about 260 s. The second can be seen better when focusing on the majority of traces, as done in Fig. 10(b) and (d). They show that the speed is – in addition to the continuous progress towards a correct value – oscillating with an amplitude of 2 s. The reason could be the dawdling, as discussed for vehicles approaching a major intersection. But, when looking at the same run with a dawdling value set to zero, as visualized in Fig. 10(c) and (d), some oscillations are still visible. The third peculiarity is an overestimation shortly before the link is reached. At the current time, these effects cannot be explained.

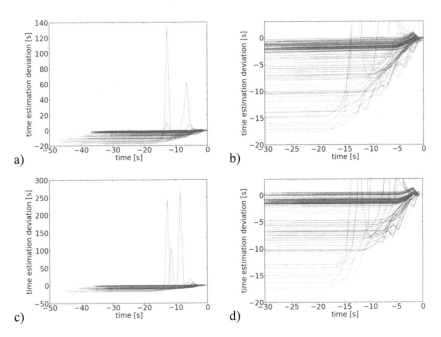

**Fig. 10.** Deviations of the estimated time from their final counterpart for arrival at an intersection (red) and leaving an intersection (blue). Top: with default dawdling, bottom: with no dawdling, left: the complete figure, right: focus on the majority of approaches. Values are for vehicles which have yield (do not have the right of way). In all plots red and blue carves are intermixed evenly (Color figure online).

# 4   Summary

The currently implemented model for right-of-way rules at intersections was presented. Important features for the detailed simulation of intersection dynamics such as the computation of approach speeds, the computation of safe acceptance gaps, and the prevention of jammed intersections were described. Furthermore, it was shown that the model is suitable for simulations with configurable time steps. Preliminary validation results of the approaching behavior were presented. These will be part of a larger validation effort which is planned for all of the simulation models implemented in SUMO.

# References

1. Behrisch, M., Bieker, L., Erdmann, J., Krajzewicz, D.: SUMO – simulation of urban mobility: an overview. In: SIMUL 2011, The Third International Conference on Advances in System Simulation (2011)
2. DLR and contributors: SUMO homepage. http://sumo.sourceforge.net/ (2013)
3. Krajzewicz, D.: Traffic simulation with SUMO–simulation of urban mobility. In: Barceló, J. (ed.) Fundamentals of Traffic Simulation. International Series in Operations Research & Management Science, vol. 145. Springer, New York (2010). ISBN 978-1-4419-6141-9
4. Krajzewicz, D., Erdmann, J.: Road intersection model in SUMO. In: 1st SUMO User Conference - SUMO 2013, pp. 212–220 (2013). ISSN 1866-721X
5. SUMO source code corresponding to this document. http://sumo-sim.org/trac.wsgi/browser/tags/v0_20_0/sumo/src
6. StVo §11, Bundesgesetzblatt Teil I, Nr. 12 (2013)
7. California Driver Handbook, p. 18
8. Krauß, S., Wagner, P., Gawron, C.: Metastable states in a microscopic model of traffic flow. Phys. Rev. E **55**, 5597–5602 (1997)

# Basic Driving Dynamics of Cyclists

Erik Andresen[1]([⊠]), Mohcine Chraibi[2], Armin Seyfried[1,2],
and Felix Huber[1]

[1] Department of Civil Engineering, Faculty D, University of Wuppertal,
Pauluskirchstr. 7, 42285 Wuppertal, Germany
{e.andresen, huber}@uni-wuppertal.de
[2] Jülich Supercomputing Center, Forschungszentrum Jülich GmbH,
52425 Jülich, Germany
{chraibi, seyfried}@uni-wuppertal.de

**Abstract.** In this work we introduce the Necessary-Deceleration-Model (NDM) which is a car-following-model developed to investigate driving behavior of bicycles. For this purpose the derivation of the mathematical description of the NDM is investigated. For the sake of calibration and validation of the model, several experiments are performed. The results of the experiments are presented and examined. Finally, the limits and possibilities of the NDM are discussed.

**Keywords:** Driving dynamics · Bicycles · Car-following-model · Ordinary differential equations

## 1 Introduction

Recently people's awareness of the environment changed due to the global warming and lack of resources. Many people use their bicycle not only as a leisure activity but also in order to reach their work site [8]. Therefore it is not surprising that the popularity of cycling has grown in the last years and is still increasing. In Central Europe more and more tracks for cyclists are built or are still in planning. Furthermore, the use of e-bikes and pedelecs increased, such that special routes for fast bicycles are in consideration.

In some situations, where special routes for bicycles are missing, cyclists must use together with cars the same route. However, neither traffic systems in which only cyclists are involved nor heterogeneous traffic systems with cars, motorcycles, bicycles, e-bikes and pedestrians are well investigated [7, 11, 12].

A long-range goal is to find and determine characteristics which are necessary for planning and designing roadway facilities and for controlling and regulating traffic flow [10].

In order to achieve this goal we investigate basic driving dynamics with help of the Necessary-Deceleration-Model scrutinized in the following sections.

© Springer-Verlag Berlin Heidelberg 2014
M. Behrisch et al. (Eds.): SUMO 2013, LNCS 8594, pp. 18–32, 2014.
DOI: 10.1007/978-3-662-45079-6_2

## 2  The Necessary-Deceleration-Model

### 2.1  Miscellaneous

The Necessary-Deceleration-Model (NDM) is a uni-dimensional car-following-model continuous in space especially designed to simulate the driving behavior of bicycles.

Like car-following-models in general [1, 2], the NDM describes the driving behavior of a vehicle from its own perspective while it is in a traffic system. That means the state variables of each vehicle are updated at each time step and determined by mathematical regularities (see Fig. 1).

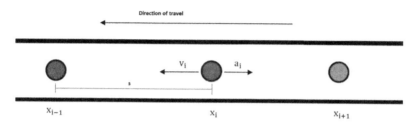

**Fig. 1.** Spatial coordinate, velocity and acceleration of a virtual vehicle in a uni-dimensional car-following-model while it is in a breaking progress.

A driver, regardless of the type of vehicle he uses, has a desired speed which he tries to reach if there is no slower vehicle or obstacle in front of him.

In case there is a slower moving predecessor, the driver will decrease his speed by decelerating until his speed is aligned to the speed of the predecessor. The amount of the deceleration depends on the current headway $s$ [1–3] and the current difference of the velocities $\Delta v (= v_{i-1} - v_i)$ between the considered driver and his predecessor [1, 3, 4, 9]. Considering s and $\Delta v$ in every time step the deceleration has to be high enough to avoid collisions [1, 4, 9].

As all vehicles can only decrease their speed with a certain maximum deceleration, the driver has to maintain a safety distance $d(v)$ depending on his own speed [1, 3].

### 2.2  Derivation of the NDM

The NDM consists of three components acc, $dec_1$ and $dec_2$ representing the acceleration and the deceleration of a vehicle. As the NDM is discrete in time, the velocity and the spatial coordinate of a driver in the next time step are numerically calculated by means of an adequate numerical solver and considering the superposition of the acceleration and deceleration terms as expressed in the following equations:

$$x(t + \Delta t) = x(t) + v(t) \cdot \Delta t, \tag{1}$$

$$v(t + \Delta t) = v(t) + (acc + \min(dec_1 + dec_2, b_{max})) \cdot \Delta t, \tag{2}$$

with: $\Delta t =$ a time constant.

**Acceleration.** The first term $acc$ is representing the free acceleration of a vehicle until it reaches its desired speed $v_0$. For this purpose the following expression [5] is used:

$$acc = \frac{v_0 - v}{\tau}. \tag{3}$$

The relaxation time $\tau$ regulates how fast a vehicle can accelerate to its desired speed.

If a driver falls below the safety distance $d(v)$ it is not necessary and furthermore not useful for him to continue accelerating. That means the term $acc$ is only supposed to be effective if the vehicle's current distance $s$ is bigger than the safety distance $d(v)$:

$$acc = \begin{cases} 0, & s \leq d(v) \\ \dfrac{v_0 - v}{\tau}, & s > d(v). \end{cases} \tag{4}$$

For simplicity the safety distance $d(v)$ is assumed to be linearly velocity-dependent:

$$d(v) = s_0 + l + T \cdot v, \tag{5}$$

with:

$s_0$ = distance between two standing vehicles (see Fig. 2),
$T$ = constant of proportionality,
$l$ = length of the considered vehicle.

**Deceleration.** As mentioned earlier a driver has to decrease his speed with a deceleration that is high enough to avoid a collision with an obstacle in front of him. For this purpose we introduce the fundamental physical equation

$$s_{nec} = \frac{(\Delta v)^2}{2b}. \tag{6}$$

In this case $s_{nec}$ is representing the necessary braking distance of a vehicle to avoid a collision. It depends on the square of the relative speed if the vehicle decreases its speed with a certain deceleration $b$. If we rearrange Eq. (6) to

$$b_{nec} = \frac{(\Delta v)^2}{2s} \tag{7}$$

we obtain the necessary deceleration $b_{nec}$ to avoid a collision depending on the current difference of the speeds of the considered vehicle and his predecessor and the current headway $s$.

However, $s$ describes the distance between the centers of two vehicles. As vehicles of all type have a physical length, we need to increase the braking distance, so that the foremost point of a vehicle does not touch the tail of the front vehicle. Furthermore it is common to preserve some security distance between the vehicles even if all of them had come to a standstill. Taking these considerations into account we obtain from Eq. (7)

$$b_{nec} = \frac{(\Delta v)^2}{2\left(s - 2 \cdot \frac{l}{2} - s_0\right)} \qquad (8)$$

as the necessary deceleration for a vehicle to avoid a collision and to keep a certain distance to the front vehicle after the braking process (see Fig. 2). Hereby we assume that all vehicles have the same length $l$.

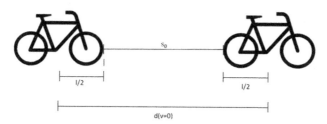

**Fig. 2.** Aspired distance $d(v)$ between two standing vehicles.

As the necessary deceleration $b_{nec}$ is expected to be high enough to avoid headways below $s_0 + l$, there is for now no need to consider the case $s - s_0 - l \leq 0$.

Since no type of vehicle is able to slow down with a deceleration higher than a certain maximum, we have to consider the limitation of the necessary deceleration $b_{nec}$ to a maximum $b_{max}$. We obtain:

$$b_{nec} = \min\left(\frac{(\Delta v)^2}{2(s - l - s_0)}, b_{max}\right). \qquad (9)$$

Because of the limitation of $b_{nec}$ to the maximum $b_{max}$ the minimal distance $s_0 + l$ can be undercut in dangerous braking situations. However, using realistic values for the model parameters these undercuts are negligibly small. Hence, they can be tolerated.

To distinguish $b_{nec}$ from further, later introduced, deceleration terms we define:

$$dec_1 := b_{nec}. \qquad (10)$$

The NDM is already up to now able to simulate plausible driving behaviour of vehicles in the three fundamental traffic situations (free accelerating, moving in a group, approaching an obstacle) of the longitudinal dynamic [1], except for the following situation:

As a driver approaches his predecessor, he decreases his speed until it is aligned to the front vehicle's speed. Assuming the considered driver has to decelerate with a high deceleration, so that he undercuts the safety distance, there is no deceleration which let him fall back to maintain the safety distance again. Because $dec_1 = 0$ if the velocities of two considered vehicles are aligned, an additional deceleration term must be considered, namely:

$$dec_2 = \frac{b_{max}}{(l - d(v))^2} \cdot (s - d(v))^2. \tag{11}$$

The second deceleration term $dec_2$ is only effective if $s \leq d(v)$.

The fact that $dec_2$ vanishes if $s = d(v)$ guarantees a continuous deceleration in every situation.

Since the distance between two drivers quickly increases if the front one is vastly faster, it is only necessary for the second deceleration term to be effective if the difference between the velocities is lower than a constant parameter $\epsilon$. We obtain:

$$dec_2 = \begin{cases} \dfrac{b_{max}}{(l - d(v))^2} \cdot (s - d(v))^2, & s \leq d(v); \Delta v \leq \epsilon \\ 0, & \text{otherwise.} \end{cases} \tag{12}$$

As $dec_1$ and $dec_2$ can be effective simultaneously in certain situations we have to limit their summation to the maximum possible deceleration $b_{max}$ due to the previously mentioned fact, that a vehicle can only decrease its speed with a deceleration not more than a certain maximum.

## 3   Calibration and Validation of the NDM

### 3.1   Miscellaneous

For calibration and validation of the NDM we evaluate the bicycle experiments dated on May, 6th 2012 in Wuppertal, Germany performed by the University of Wuppertal in cooperation with Jülich Supercomputing Center. About 30 participants aged 7–66 years were involved. Two of the participants used an e-bike.

Using the videos filmed by two cameras that overlooked the whole area of the car park (see Fig. 3) we were able to extract the trajectories of the cyclists. As part of the test runs two different types of experiments were carried out.

The first experimental run called *Single Experiments* was performed to investigate the individual behaviour of cyclists while accelerating. For this purpose participants have to increase their speed from zero until the desired speed is reached.

We carried out the second experimental run called *Group Experiments* to investigate the collective driving behaviour of cyclists while moving in a group. There for a settled number of cyclists are supposed to drive through an oval track simultaneously without being allowed to overtake (see Fig. 3). The participants were told to drive normally without haste.

### 3.2   Data Analysis Methods

The measuring range was located at one of the straight lines of the oval track. Its length $\Delta x$ has been set to 20 m.

**Fig. 3.** Experimental set-up (*Group Experiment*) with 33 participants.

The *Single Experiments* or rather the individual acceleration progress of a cyclist took place in the measuring area without exception. For every recorded time step $j$ of an acceleration phase we calculate the current speed of the regarded vehicle $i$ (see Eq. 13).

$$v_{i,j} = \frac{x_j - x_{j-1}}{t_j - t_{j-1}}.$$ (13)

For the sake of measuring the density and velocity of the system while performing the Group Experiments we make use of the following data analysis methods:

For every pass of a bicycle through the measuring area $(t \in [t_{in}, t_{out}])$ its mean speed is determined by using Eq. (14).

$$v_i = \frac{\Delta x}{t_{out} - t_{in}} [6].$$ (14)

Additionally at every time step a bicycle is located in the measuring area the amount of bicycles $N$ in the area is counted. We use Eq. (15) to obtain the mean density assigned to each participant passing through the measuring range. (In Comparison with [6] Eq. (15) is changed for our purpose to analysis discrete one-dimensional data.)

$$\rho_i = \frac{1}{(t_{out} - t_{in}) \cdot \Delta x} \cdot \sum_{t_i = t_{in}}^{t_{out}} N_{i,t_i} \quad [6]. \tag{15}$$

Taking into account the mean speed and mean density assigned to a pass through of a vehicle as a tuple we are able to set up the velocity-density and flow-density relation. The flow $J_i$ is calculated by Eq. (16).

$$J_i = v_i \cdot \rho_i. \tag{16}$$

For the sake of investigating the velocity-headway relation (see Fig. 6) we calculate the velocity with the aid of Eq. (14) and make use of the following headway definition:

$$d_i = \frac{1}{\rho_i}. \tag{17}$$

### 3.3  Driving Behaviour While Accelerating

**Experimental Results.** The average desired speed of the participants is about 4.3 m/s (corresponds 15.5 km/h) (see Fig. 4). The standard deviation of the desired velocity

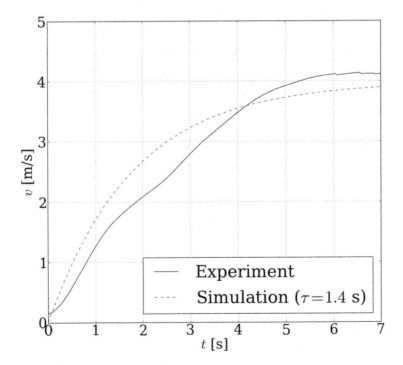

**Fig. 4.** Free flow acceleration of real cyclists and cyclists simulated using the NDM.

resulted in 0.57 m/s (corresponds 2.05 km/h). On average it takes 20–25 m to accelerate to the desired speed and the duration of the acceleration phase is about 7 s.

**Calibration.** As shown in Fig. 4 the exponential acceleration that emerges from Eq. (3) is in good agreement with the empirical acceleration process of the participants. Therefore, the model parameter $v_0$ is assumed as Gaussian-distributed with a mean value of 4.3 m/s and a standard deviation of 0.57 m/s. The parameter $\tau$ is set to 1.4 s.

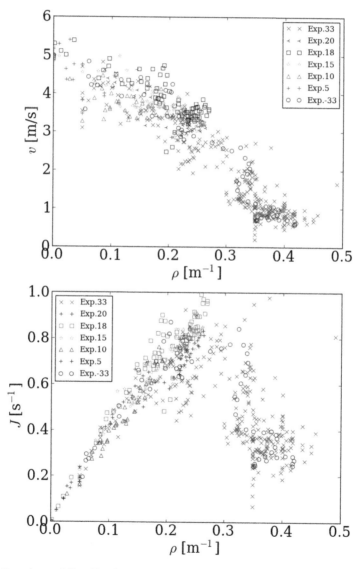

**Fig. 5.** Experimental flow/density-velocity relation (Exp. -33 = Exp. 33 (anti-clockwise)).

### 3.4    Driving Behaviour While Moving in a Group

**Experimental Results.** By analyzing the results of several experimental runs of the *Group Experiment* with various numbers of participants the fundamental diagrams can be set up. For this purpose experimental runs with 5, 7, 10, 15, 18, 20 and 33 participants have been performed. In the run with 33 vehicles the drivers had to move clock- and anti-clockwise. The length of the circuit was set to 86 m.

The following characteristics of driving behaviour can be extracted from Fig. 5.

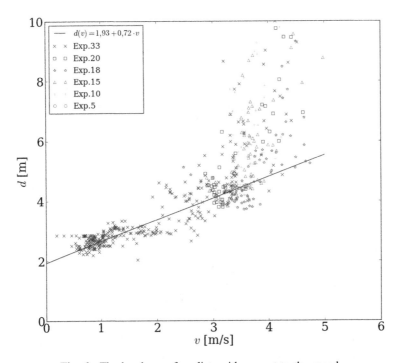

**Fig. 6.** The headway of cyclists with respect to the speed.

**Table 1.** Adapted model parameters of the NDM calibrated by using the measurements of the bicycle experiments.

| Model parameter | Value |
| --- | --- |
| $v_0$ | Gauss-distributed (mean-value: 15.5 km/h; standard deviation: 2 km/h) |
| $\tau$ | 1.4 s |
| $T$ | 0.72 s |
| $s_0$ | 0.2 m |
| $l$ | 1.73 m |
| $b_{max}$ | −5.5 m/s |
| $\epsilon$ | 1.8 km/h |

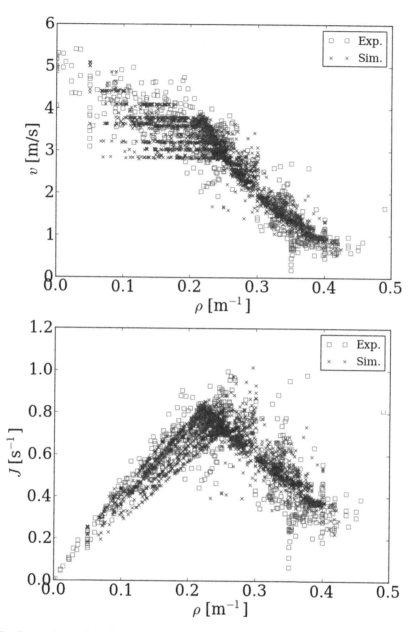

**Fig. 7.** Comparison of the fundamental diagrams of the experimental runs and the simulation runs (N = 1, 2, 3, 4, 5, 8, 10, 15, 18, 20, 22, 25, 28, 30, 33) performed by the NDM using the model parameter listed in Table 1 and the numerical integration interval $\Delta t = 0.01s$.

The maximum flow of ca. 0.8 s$^{-1}$ is located at the density of $\sim 0.25$ m$^{-1}$. By density regions below this density, the mean speed of drivers is mainly determined by the speed of the slowest one, since he is the only one who can freely accelerate, respectively, moving with his desired speed. Above the density 0.25 m$^{-1}$ the slowest driver is hindered by his predecessor as well, that is, the speed of the system is no more determined by the desired speed of the slowest vehicle.

**Calibration.** We already could determine the real values of the desired speed and the relaxation time of the acceleration progress to calibrate the NDM by investigating the *Single Experiments*. Furthermore we obtained the mean length of a bicycle (1.73 m) by surveying all bicycles before starting the experiments.

Adapting the results of experiments according to the maximum deceleration of bicycles performed by [13] we set the parameter $b_{max}$ to 5.5 m/s$^2$.

We make use of the results of the experimental runs to calibrate the remaining model parameters. To adjust the parameters $s_0$ and $T$ we build up the headway-velocity relation of the experiment (see Fig. 6).

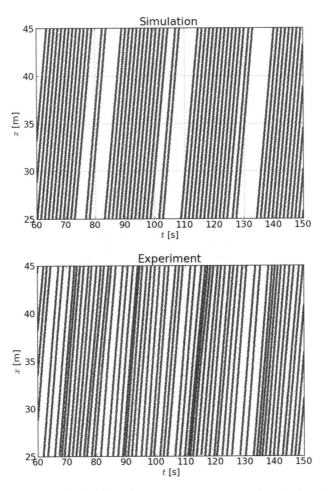

**Fig. 8.** Comparison of the trajectories (N = 15) of the experimental and the simulation runs performed by the NDM using the model parameter listed in Table 1 and the numerical integration interval $\Delta t = 0.01s$.

We assume that only the velocity-headway relation located lower than the velocity of the slowest driver, namely ~3.35 m/s, is relevant to calibrate the parameters of the safety distance. That means we solely regard the systems in which the density is high enough so that every driver is hindered to drive freely by his predecessor. Hence, the distance between two vehicles can be understood as the safety distance in this case.

Using two tuples of the headway-velocity relation taken from the area below the velocity of ~3.35 m/s we fit a linear function which represents the safety distance (see Fig. 6). Note that the linear function can only approximately describe the safety distance. However, for the sake of calibration our model parameters this procedure is sufficient.

The linear relationship of the safety distance and the speed is found to be as:

$$d(v) = 1.93 + 0.72 \cdot v \tag{18}$$

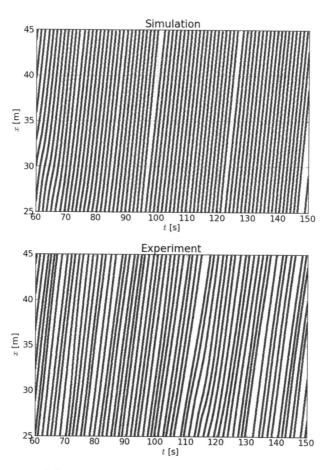

**Fig. 9.** Comparison of the trajectories N = 20 (Adjustment of the parameters: see Caption Fig. 8).

Accordingly we can set the parameter $T$ to 0.72 s. As the safety distance is described by $s_0 + l$ and we already have measured the length of a vehicle $l$ as 1.73 m (see above) we notice 0.2 m to calibrate the parameter $s_0$.

We have calibrated every single model parameter by using experimental data except for the parameter $\epsilon$. We set $\epsilon$ to 1.8 km/h as an preliminary estimate.

The adapted model parameters are summarized in Table 1.

**Validation.** Considering the calibrated model parameters of the NDM (Table 1) the relation of velocity, density and flow can be realistically reproduced by the NDM (see Fig. 7).

The qualitative behaviour of cyclists is investigated by comparing the experimental and simulated trajectories of selected systems. In Fig. 8 we show the trajectories of a

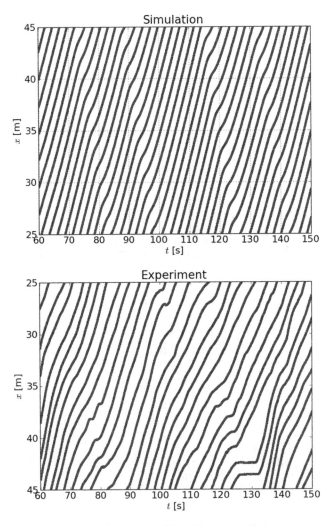

**Fig. 10.** Comparison of the trajectories N = 33 (Adjustment of the parameters: see Caption Fig. 8).

run with 15 participants. In this system the group building or rather queue building of the cyclists is predominating. There is at least one driver who can drive freely.

We see this driving behaviour as well in the simulation as in the experiment.

By comparing the subfigures of Fig. 9 we notice that the cyclists of the experimental and the simulated run with 20 drivers show similar patterns again. The system is predominated by an equal distribution of the participants. The drivers still drive with a constant speed.

In Fig. 10 the trajectories of the system with 33 participants are shown. By investigating the figure we notice the occurrence of congestions. That is, although the drivers do not come to a standstill most of the times they have to vary their speed partly noticeably. Again, the simulated and the real cyclists show these patterns.

## 4   Conclusion, Limits and Possibilities of the NDM

Since the NDM is developed by using fundamental physical relationships, the model parameters reflect physical characteristics of the driver or the vehicle. The NDM can model plausible driving behaviour in the three traffic situations of the longitudinal dynamic (free accelerating, moving in a group, approaching an obstacle).

By using the calibrated parameters, collisions do not occur. The driving dynamics responds only slightly to changes in the model parameters. Figures 4, 5, 6, 7, 8, 9, and 10 show that the model provides reasonable quantitative and qualitative results when plausible values for the model parameters are used. Especially the comparison of the fundamental diagrams (see Fig. 7) shows that the NDM can model realistic driving behaviour of cyclists moving in a group. Furthermore, as seen in Fig. 4 the NDM is able to replicate the free acceleration progress of cyclists.

By comparing the trajectories of simulated and real drivers (see Figs. 8, 9, and 10) we notice similar behavioural features in various closed traffic systems with different densities.

Although originally the NDM has been developed to model the dynamics of cyclists in a traffic system, it is technically possible to simulate the dynamics of cars or shared-used routes as well. However, a thoroughly investigation of the NDM to investigate the exact dynamics of the mentioned systems is scheduled for future works.

**Acknowledgements.** We would like to thank Wolfgang Mehner and Maik Boltes working at Jülich Research Center for filming and extracting the trajectories of the bicycle experiments dated on 6th May 2012. Furthermore we would like to thank all the participants and helpers who were involved at the bicycle experiments and remain disciplined, so that excellent results of the experimental runs could be achieved.

## References

1. Treiber, M., Kesting, A.: Verkehrsdynamik und –simulation. Springer Lehrbuch, Heidelberg (2010)
2. Bando, M., Hasebe, K., Nakayama, A., Shibata, A., Sugiyama, Y.: Dynamical model of traffic congestion and numerical simulation. Phys. Rev. E **51**, 1035–1042 (1995)

3. Gipps, P.G.: A behavourial car-following model for computer simulation. Transp. Res. B Methodol. **15**, 105–111 (1981)
4. Treiber, M., Hennecke, A., Helbing, D.: Congested traffic states in empirical observations and microscopic simulations. Phys. Rev. E **62**, 1805–1824 (2000)
5. Pipes, L.A.: An operational analysis of traffic dynamics. J. Appl. Phys. **24**, 274 (1953)
6. Zhang, J., Klingsch, W., Schadschneider, A., Seyfried, A.: Transitions in pedestrian fundamental diagrams of straight corridors and T-junctions. J. Stat. Mech. Theor. Exp. **2011**(06), P06004 (2011)
7. Faghri, A., Egyhaziova, E.: Development of a computer simulation model of mixed motor vehicle and bicycle traffic on an urban road network. Transp. Res. Rec.: Safety and Human Performance, **1674**(1999), 86–93 (1999)
8. Gould, G., Karner, A.: Modeling bicycle facility operation: a cellular automaton approach. Transp. Res. Rec.: J. Trans. Res. Board, **2140**, 157–164 (2009)
9. Jiang, R., Wu, Q., Zhu, Z.: Full velocity difference model for a car-following theory. Phys. Rev. E **64**, 017101 (2001)
10. Navin, F.P.D.: Bicycle traffic flow characteristics: experimental results and comparisons. ITE J. **64**, 31–36 (1994)
11. Arasan, V.T., Koshy, R.Z.: Methodology for modeling highly heterogeneous traffic flow. J. Transp. Eng. **131**, 544–551 (2005)
12. Minh, C.C.: Kazushi Sano and Shoji Matsumoto (2005) The speed flow and headway analyses of motorcycle traffic. J. East. Asia Soc. Transp. Stud. **6**, 1496–1508 (2005)
13. Bäumler, H.: Bremsverzögerung von modernen Fahrrädern 2.3.4., Verkehrsunfall und Fahrzeugtechnik, Fachblatt für Kraftfahrzeug 47.11:347 (2009)

# Implementation of an Energy Model and a Charging Infrastructure in SUMO

Tamás Kurczveil$^{(\boxtimes)}$, Pablo Álvarez López, and Eckehard Schnieder

Institute for Traffic Safety and Automation Engineering,
Technische Universität Braunschweig, Langer Kamp 8,
38106 Brunswick, Germany
{kurczveil,schnieder}@iva.ing.tu-bs.de

**Abstract.** Future traffic that will be accompanied by higher alternative drive concepts will pose as a challenge when it comes to corresponding energy systems, coordination of operations, and communication interfaces, such as needed for data acquisition and billing. On one hand, the increasing attractiveness of electric vehicles will inevitably lead to the development and testing of compatible technologies; on the other, these will need to be conformed to existing systems, when integrating them into the prevailing infrastructure and traffic. Funded by the German Federal Ministry of Transport, Building and Urban Development, an inductive vehicle charging system and a compatible prototype bus fleet shall be integrated into Braunschweig's traffic infrastructure in the scope of the project *emil* (Elektromobilität mittels induktiver Ladung – electric mobility via inductive charging). This paper describes the functional implementations in SUMO that are required by the methodic approach for the evaluation of novel charging infrastructures by means of traffic simulation.

**Keywords:** Traffic simulation · Urban traffic · Inductive energy transfer · Public transportation · Vehicle model

## 1 Introduction

The prospective post-oil era and rising fuel prices have lately resulted in several global trends towards alternative drive technologies. The main advantage of gasoline fuel over other energy carriers is its high specific energy of up to 44.0 MJ/kg. Current projections for the development of equally convenient alternative energy storages go far beyond 2030. Thus, the utilization of alternative energy sources, such as the electrochemical energy stored in Lithium-Ion batteries (0.5 MJ/kg), will result in high vehicle masses and/or low ranges for the coming decades [1, 2].

Measures that aim to counter these deficits include the application of light-weight materials, energy/time-optimal routing, intelligent control of and communication with traffic light-signal systems, and government regulations that introduce (operational, financial and/or infrastructural) incentives for buyers of vehicles with alternative drive concepts.

The German Federal Ministry of Transport, Building and Urban Development (BMVBS) has therefore granted the funding of the project *emil* (Elektromobilität

© Springer-Verlag Berlin Heidelberg 2014
M. Behrisch et al. (Eds.): SUMO 2013, LNCS 8594, pp. 33–43, 2014.
DOI: 10.1007/978-3-662-45079-6_3

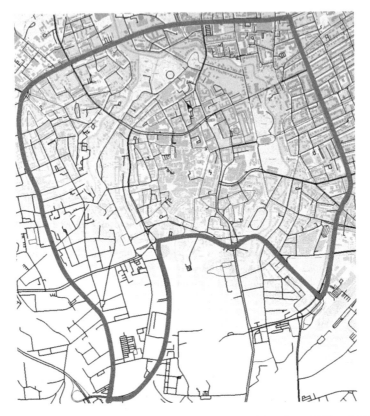

**Fig. 1.** Braunschweig's urban road network with the route of bus lines M19 and M29 (broad line) © OpenStreetMap-Contributors

mittels induktiver Ladung – electric mobility via inductive charging). It includes the evaluative implementation of an inductive energy transfer system for public transportation and a compatible prototype bus fleet in the city of Braunschweig. The bus lines in question are the M29 and M19 that circle the city center counter-clockwise and clockwise, respectively. They carry the highest percentage of Braunschweig's publicly transported passengers with a high frequency from and to major traffic nodes and landmarks such as the central train station and the university. Figure 1 illustrates Braunschweig's urban road network.

The goal of the project *emil* is to analyze and optimize the operation and economic feasibility of an inductive electric charging system and to develop suitable operating strategies. One focus of research lies in the analysis of integrative aspects that allow for the common utilization of the charging and road transport infrastructure by public and private transport with minimum obstruction of public and total traffic. After outlining the methodic approach for these analyses, the implementations in SUMO shall be described that allow for its utilization in urban traffic optimization.

## 2  Methodic Approach

The goal of possible optimization measures (e.g. via genetic algorithms) lies in finding an optimum of the considered system in regard of the energy consumed. This evaluation requires a suitable simulation tool that allows the implementation of custom traffic scenarios, including traffic demand, a charging infrastructure, customized vehicles, prioritization, and different light-signal schedules. Additionally, it needs to generate an output of the required energy of individual road traffic participants and the entire system as the desired optimization criterion.

Since no simulation tools exist that allow all the mentioned requirement to be modeled, the best choice for this task is the traffic simulation tool SUMO (Simulation of Urban MObility), due to its open source character and high compatibility with numerous data sources, including many commercially available traffic simulation tools [3, 4]. Its development was initiated by the Institute of Transportation Systems of the German Aerospace Center (DLR), in 2001. It has evolved into a simulation tool, high in features, functionality and interfaces. Even though instantiated vehicles follow a simplified behavior, traffic simulation tools like SUMO allow the realistic replication of prevailing traffic in arbitrary road networks.

The intended approach in the scope of this project is to model current representative traffic scenarios that take into account the existing infrastructure, a time-varying traffic demand model (differentiating between representative peak and nonbusy periods), and light-signal schedules [5]. Meanwhile, the implementation of new functionalities in SUMO on the system-function level will allow for the instantiation of inductive charging stations and compatible vehicles. Operation parameters will have to be identified and/or set for the inductive charging system and traffic demand, to create a representative scenario for Braunschweig's urban traffic. Figure 2 depicts the above described method, highlighting interfaces between SUMO's current functionalities, required additional functionalities, and an external optimization framework.

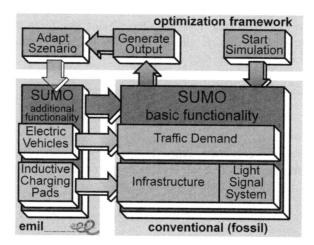

**Fig. 2.** Project structure with interfaces between basic functionalities (gray), additional functionalities (green), and an optimization framework (blue) (Color figure online)

# 3   State of the Art and Vehicle Model

In order to generate an output about the consumed energy, an energy model will have to be implemented for instantiated vehicle objects. Numerous methods, functions and approaches exist that perform traffic quality assessment calculations, giving feedback about its characteristics. Implemented functionalities in SUMO include the vehicle- and lane-based HBEFA-emission [6] and HARMONOISE-noise [7] calculation and the corresponding generation of a suitable output.

In order to allow energy assessments and subsequent optimization, an additional framework has also been developed by Maia et al. [8]. The work is based on a sophisticated vehicle model that takes into account mechanic and electric vehicle parameters and calculates the variation of the depth of discharge between discrete time steps. If a vehicle's movement requires a higher torque than its defined maximum, recalculations of the vehicle speed and acceleration take place in order to comply with the constraints of its components. The depth of discharge is subsequently calculated using an electrical traction model.

With the aim to enhance computation time, this paper presents the implementation of a similar vehicle model, which merely focuses on energy as the simulation output and reduces the complexity of required calculations. Additionally, this model evaluates the energetic state and calculates variations in energy content of corresponding vehicles without affecting their driving behavior. Additional benefits of this model include fewer required input arguments for instantiating vehicle objects.

## 3.1   Vehicle Energy Model

The change of one vehicle's energy content can be calculated by summing its kinetic, potential, and rotational energy gain components from one discrete time step to the following, and subtracting the losses caused by different resistance components [9]. The vehicle's energy $E_{veh}[k]$ at the discrete time step $k$ can thus be calculated by Eq. 1, with the known variables vehicle mass $m$, time variant vehicle speed $v[k]$, gravity acceleration $g$, time variant vehicle altitude $h[k]$, and moment of inertia of internal rotating elements $J_{int}$.

$$
\begin{aligned}
E_{veh}[k] &= E_{kin}[k] + E_{pot}[k] + E_{rot,int}[k] \\
&= \frac{m}{2} \cdot v^2[k] + m \cdot g \cdot h[k] + \frac{J_{int}}{2} \cdot v^2[k]
\end{aligned}
\tag{1}
$$

In consideration of energy losses $\Delta E_{loss}[k]$ caused by air, rolling, and curve resistance and constant consumers (e.g. air conditioning), the energy gain between time steps $k$ and $k + 1$ can be calculated by Eq. 2.

$$
\Delta E_{gain}[k] = E_{veh}[k + 1] - E_{veh}[k] - \Delta E_{loss}[k]
\tag{2}
$$

The energy loss is made up of the components in Eq. 3, with the variables air density $\rho_{air}$, vehicle front surface area $A_{veh}$, air drag coefficient $c_w$, covered distance $s[k]$, rolling resistance coefficient $c_{roll}$, centripetal force $F_{rad}$, curve resistance coefficient $c_{rad}$, and the (average) power of constant consumers $P_{const}$ [9].

$$\Delta E_{loss}[k] = \Delta E_{air}[k] + \Delta E_{roll}[k] + \Delta E_{curve}[k] + \Delta E_{const}[k]$$

$$\Delta E_{air}[k] = \frac{1}{2}\rho_{air} \cdot A_{veh} \cdot c_{w} \cdot v^2[k] \cdot |\Delta s[k]|$$

$$\Delta E_{roll}[k] = c_{roll} \cdot m \cdot g \cdot |\Delta s[k]| \tag{3}$$

$$\Delta E_{curve}[k] = c_{rad} \cdot \frac{m \cdot v^2[k]}{r[k]} \cdot |\Delta s[k]|$$

$$\Delta E_{const}[k] = P_{const} \cdot \Delta t$$

Depending on its sign, $\Delta E_{gain}[k]$ is the amount of energy the vehicle has consumed or regained resulting from its movement. The variation of the energy contained in the vehicle's battery can further be calculated by Eqs. 4 and 5 by introducing constant efficiency factors for recuperation $\eta_{recup}(\Delta E_{gain}[k] > 0)$ and propulsion $\eta_{prop}(\Delta E_{gain}[k] < 0)$.

$$E_{Bat}[k+1] = E_{Bat}[k] + \Delta E_{gain}[k] \cdot \eta_{recup} \tag{4}$$

$$E_{Bat}[k+1] = E_{Bat}[k] + \Delta E_{gain}[k] \cdot \eta_{prop}^{-1} \tag{5}$$

### 3.2 Vehicle Charging Model

For the purpose of evaluating a charging infrastructure, a new object will have to be implemented into SUMO that supplies compatible vehicles (or their batteries) with energy for their operation. The location of charging stations as well as their charging power and efficiency needs to be specifiable by the user. If a vehicle moves or stops above or within a system-specific proximity of such an infrastructure element, the energy content of its battery is charged according to Eq. 6, with charging power $P_{chrg}$, charging efficiency $\eta_{chrg}$, and duration between two discrete time steps $\Delta t$.

$$E_{Bat}[k+1] = E_{Bat}[k] + P_{chrg} \cdot \eta_{chrg} \cdot \Delta t \tag{6}$$

Following the calculations of the energy variation between two discrete time steps, the battery's energy content is limited to the user-specifiable range

$$0 \leq E_{Bat} \leq E_{Bat,max}. \tag{7}$$

Calculations of this energy model can be restricted to vehicles with $E_{Bat,max} > 0$, further reducing computing times.

### 3.3 Model Simulation and Results

For the correct dimensioning of components and layout, the technology provider Bombardier Transportation GmbH has developed a sophisticated simulation model for the variation of the battery's energy content. Since the vehicles, which are to be used in this project, are still in development, this output of this sophisticated model is the only reference for a representative parameterization. In order to show that the simplistic vehicle model presented above is capable of calculating the trend of a vehicle's energy content with adequate accuracy, it has been given the same route as input, as Bombardier's sophisticated model (Solaris Urbino 12). Figure 3 shows the vehicle's route and its topographic profile.

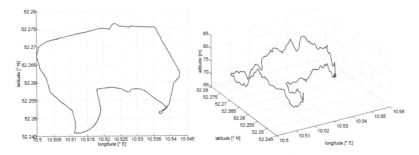

**Fig. 3.** Designated bus route (left) and its topographic profile (right)

In a subsequent step, parameters for the newly developed vehicle model in SUMO have been determined that represent the reference behavior optimally, in the sense of least-squares. The reference (blue) and parameterized (red) simulation outputs for the same route as the model input are shown in Fig. 4. The cumulated ($\Delta t = 1$s) deviation of the two simulation outputs add up to $E_{Error} = 3.3998$ kWh$^2$.

The implementation of this vehicle kinematic and charging model is described in Chap. 4.

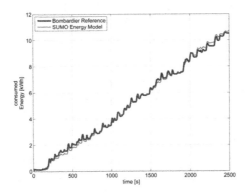

**Fig. 4.** Simulation outputs of Bombardier's reference simulation and the newly implemented energy model with an optimal parameter set

# 4  Implementation

The new implementations focus around the newly created battery device as part of the micro-simulation engine *MSDevice_Battery*. It allows the definition of vehicle types with new parameters and performs the calculations of the model described in Sect. 3.2. Modifications in the net-loading modules further allow the definition of charging stations with its relevant parameters, as described in Sect. 3.3. The modifications were made on the basis of SUMO revision 14712 and successfully validated with newer releases of SUMO.

For the calculation of the energy variation in a vehicle's battery, new parameters had to be introduced that can describe vehicle types. Table 1 lists all new parameters for vehicle type definitions. If a vehicle type is defined with one or more of the described parameter definition keys, it gets assigned to the *MSDevice_Battery* object of the respective vehicle object. If one or more parameters are missing, a default value of 0 is assigned to the corresponding vehicle parameter.

**Table 1.**  Newly introduced vehicle parameters

| Parameter | Parameter definition key | Default |
|---|---|---|
| Maximum battery capacity $E_{max}$ | "MaxBatKap" | 0 (kWh) |
| Vehicle mass $m_{veh}$ | "Mass" | 0 (kg) |
| Front surface area $A_{veh}$ | "FrontSurfaceArea" | 0 (m$^2$) |
| Air drag coefficient $c_w$ | "AirDragCoefficient" | 0 |
| Mom. of inertia of int. rot. elements $J_{int}$ | "InternalMomentOfInertia" | 0 (kg·m$^2$) |
| Radial drag coefficient $c_{rad}$ | "RadialDragCoefficient" | 0 |
| Rolling resistance coefficient $c_{roll}$ | "RollDragCoefficient" | 0 |
| Avg. power of consumers $P_{const}$ | "ConstantPowerIntake" | 0 (kW) |
| Drive efficiency $\eta_{prop}$ | "PropulsionEfficiency" | 0 |
| Recuperation efficiency $\eta_{recup}$ | "RecuperationEfficiency" | 0 |

The basic structure of bus stops was used for the implementation of charging stations. A new charging station class *MSChrgStn* was created and the netload modules were extended to parse for charging station definitions. If one is found, a charging station is built according to the parameters listed in Table 2.

**Table 2.**  Charging station initialization

| Parameter | Parameter definition key |
|---|---|
| Charging station ID | "id" |
| Charging power $P_{chrg}$ | "power" |
| Charging efficiency $\eta_{chrg}$ | "efficiency" |
| Lane of the charging station location | "lane" |
| Begin position in the specified lane | "startPos" |
| End position in the specified lane | "endPos" |

The specified charging station objects are then added to the network class. If a compatible vehicle is located within the specified dimensions (lane, startPos, endPos) of a charging station, its battery state is updated according to the specified charging station parameters (charging power $P_{chrg}$, efficiency $\eta_{chrg}$) and Eq. 6. For graphical representation of charging stations in the graphical user interface, a new (optional) class *GUIChrgStn* was added. If used, charging stations have an individual representation in the SUMO GUI.

### 4.1  Configuration

Vehicle Types with the described parameters can be configured according to the syntax shown in Listing 1.

**Listing 1:** Syntax for the configuration of vehicle types with the described vehicle parameters

```
<vType    accel="1.0"    decel="1.0"    id="ElectricBus"    length="12"
maxSpeed="100.0" sigma="0.0" minGap="2.5" color="1,1,1">
    <param key="MaxBatKap" value="2000"/>
    <param key="Mass" value="10000"/>
    <param key="FrontSurfaceArea" value="5"/>
    <param key="AirDragCoefficient" value="0.6"/>
    <param key="InternalMomentOfInertia" value="0.01"/>
    <param key="RadialDragCoefficient" value="0.5"/>
    <param key="RollDragCoefficient" value="0.01"/>
    <param key="ConstantPowerIntake" value="100"/>
    <param key="PropulsionEfficiency" value="0.9"/>
    <param key="RecuperationEfficiency" value="0.9"/>
</vType>
```

Using the specified id from Listing 1 ("ElectricBus"), subsequent vehicles can be specified using the standard SUMO syntax for the configuration of vehicles.

Charging stations can be specified in a similar syntax as bus stops within the tag <additional>, as show in Listing 2.

**Listing 2:** Syntax for specifying vehicle stops at charging stations

```
<additional>
    <chargingStation id="ChrgStn01" lane="D1_0" startPos="20" end-
    Pos="30" chrgpower="200" efficiency = "0.95"/>
</additional >
```

Being derived from the bus stop class *MSBusStop* the implementation of the charging station class *MSChrgStn* allows the explicit allocation of stops for vehicles at charging stations as shown in the Listing 3.

**Listing 3:** Syntax for specifying vehicle stops at charging stations

```
<vehicle depart="000" id="veh0" route="route01" type="ElectricBus">
    <stop busStop="ChrgStn01" duration="10"/>
</vehicle>
```

## 4.2    Output

Listing 4 shows the syntax for triggering the output of the battery device.

**Listing 4:** Syntax for triggering the output from the configuration

```
<output>
    <battery-output value="mysimulation.battery.xml"/>
</output>
```

The generated output of the battery device is structured in the same style as the output *VTypeProbe*, however with information on individual vehicle's battery state. An example output is show in Listing 5.

**Listing 5:** Generated output of the battery device

```
<battery-export>
    <timestep time="0.00">
        <vehicle   id="veh0"   ActBatKap="100.00"   MaxBatKap="155.00"
        speed="0.00" acceleration="0.00" route="route01" lane="D2_0" po-
        sitionOnLane="12.10" waiting="0.00"/>
        … further vehicles …
    </timestep>
    … further time steps …
</battery-export >
```

The generated output can further be reprocessed for individual purposes. For validation purposes, a scenario was created for a vehicle with the determined vehicle parameters from Sect. 3.3 driving the speed profile of the New European Driving Cycle (NEDC) with no curves and a non-regular incline of 1 %. The NEDC is a defined driving cycle (speed profile) with the goal of providing a common emission and fuel

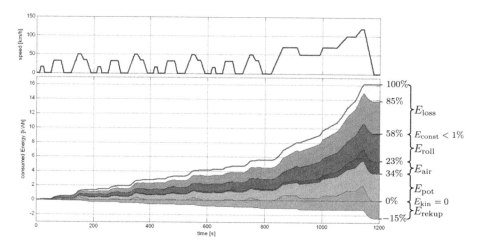

**Fig. 5.** Cumulative energy components (lower) of a vehicle when driving the speed profile (upper) of the New European Driving Cycle (NEDC) with a non-regular incline of 1 %

economy test basis for all passenger cars and is specified in UN-ECE Regulation No 101 (2012). Whereas the basis for the evaluation of the fuel economy for light trucks and commercial vehicles is specified in DIN 70030-2 (1986), the NEDC is used as a reference in the context of this work due to its widely established application. Figure 5 illustrates the resulting individual cumulative energy components derived from the battery device output, by setting individual vehicle model parameters to zero. $E_{loss}$ represents energy losses in the vehicle's drive train.

## 5    Conclusion and Outlook

The introduced vehicle energy model can be used for simulating vehicle energy consumptions with adequate accuracy and is therefore applicable for a multitude of evaluations involving energy-optimization. The identified parameter set can further be used in the resulting function package of SUMO for the instantiation of a new traffic demand model with (representative) objects of the new vehicle class, including different vehicle types. This will allow for the development of different scenarios for Braunschweig's traffic (including forecasts for electric vehicles) that can be analyzed and optimized in regard of the new inductive charging infrastructure and its participants.

The development of an optimization framework with underlying algorithms will require an additional output of the specific simulation states by producing a feedback on the energy content of relevant participants. This output could be implemented in form of a custom device or detector. Potentials for optimization lie in the optimal positioning of the charging stations along the defined bus route. The optimization criteria can not only include a desired long battery life, but also travel time by synchronizing required charging times and the predictable waiting times for the entry and exit of passengers, light-signal systems, and remaining traffic. For the identification of optimal parameter sets, the utilization of genetic algorithms is intended in the further course of the project.

Simulation results can also include the evaluation of occupancy rates at different positions within the road network. This data can be used for the design and alignment of inductive charging pads that maximize their duty cycle and thus efficiency.

By implementing different scenarios for the amount of compatible vehicles in the future, it will also be possible to determine saturation points for the amount of participating vehicles, where operational interferences and obstructions among public transportation and between public and private vehicles can be expected.

**Acknowledgements.** The project *emil* is funded by the German Federal Ministry of Transport, Building and Urban Development (Bundesministerium für Verkehr, Bau und Stadt-entwicklung – BMVBS). We hereby thank all our project partners for their continuous and kind cooperation.

Bundesministerium
für Verkehr, Bau
und Stadtentwicklung

# References

1. Winter, M.: Elektromobilität mit Lithium-Ionen-Technologie: Chancen, Herausforderungen, Alternativen. In: Proceedings of the HEV 2012. Hybrid and Electric Vehicles, Braunschweig (2012)
2. Wansart, J.: Analyse von Strategien der Automobilindustrie zur Reduktion von $CO_2$-Flottenemissionen und zur Markteinführung alternativer Antriebe: Ein systemdynamischer Ansatz am Beispiel der kalifornischen Gesetzgebung. Dissertation, Technische Universität Braunschweig, Springer Gabler, Wiesbaden (2012)
3. Behrisch, M., Bieker, L., Erdmann, J., Krajzewicz, D.: SUMO – simulation of urban mobility: an overview. In: SIMUL 2011, The Third International Conference on Advances in System Simulation, Barcelona (2011)
4. Detering, S.: Kalibrierung und Validierung von Verkehrssimulationsmodellen zur Untersuchung von Verkehrsassistenzsystemen. Dissertation, Technische Universität Braunschweig (2011)
5. Handbuch für die Bemessung von Straßenverkehrsanlagen (HBS). Forschungsgesellschaft für Straßen- und Verkehrswesen (2001)
6. Keller, M., de Haan, P.: Handbuch Emissionsfaktoren des Straßenverkehrs 2.1 – Dokumentation. INFRAS, Bern/Heidelberg/Graz/Essen (2004)
7. Nota, R., Barelds, R, van Maercke, D.: Harmonoise WP 3 Engineering method for road traffic and railway noise after validation and fine-tuning. Technical report Deliverable 18, HARMONOISE (2005)
8. Maia, R., Silva, M., Araújo, R., Nunes, U.: Electric vehicle simulator for energy consumption studies in electric mobility systems. In: 2011 IEEE Forum in Integrated and Sustainable Transportation Systems, Vienna (2011)
9. Mitschke, M., Wallentowitz, H.: Dynamik der Kraftfahrzeuge. Springer, Berlin (2004)

# Agent-Based Traffic Simulation Using SUMO and JADE: An Integrated Platform for Artificial Transportation Systems

Guilherme Soares, Zafeiris Kokkinogenis, José Luiz Macedo,
and Rosaldo J.F. Rossetti[✉]

Artificial Intelligence and Computer Science Laboratory (LIACC),
Department of Informatics Engineering (DEI) Faculty of Engineering,
University of Porto, Porto, Portugal
{guilherme.soares,zafeiris.kokkinogenis,jose.macedo,rossetti}@fe.up.pt

**Abstract.** The rapid and ever-increasing population and urban activities have imposed a massive demand to Urban Transportation Systems (UTS). These systems were not prepared for such events, so traffic congestion and defective metropolitan systems were a direct consequence of such a shortcoming. The explosion of the computing technology brought together expertise from different scientific and technical disciplines giving birth to new computing and communication paradigms. Taking advantage of modelling and simulation technologies we have devised a framework that combines the characteristics of the Multi-Agent System Development Framework, JADE, and the microscopic traffic simulator, SUMO, for the development and appraisal of multi-agent traffic solutions in contemporary transportation systems. Therefore we present a tool that can be useful to researchers and practitioners for implementing agent-based traffic control and management solutions as well as heterogeneous Artificial Societies (AS) of drivers immersed in rather realistic traffic environments.

**Keywords:** Multi-agent systems · SUMO · JADE · Artificial transportation systems

## 1 Introduction

The rapid and ever-increasing population and urban activities has imposed a massive demand to urban transportation systems. The main problem is that most of the urban areas were not prepared for such hasty development which led to weak and defective metropolitan transportation systems [9]. Efficient transportation systems are crucial to an industrialized society being its main communication infrastructure; therefore rapid and effective interventions in traffic management and planning are needed to prevent their negative impact on the city's social and economic welfare. Therefore, by using simulation and taking advantage of its characteristics we can test several possible solutions or

© Springer-Verlag Berlin Heidelberg 2014
M. Behrisch et al. (Eds.): SUMO 2013, LNCS 8594, pp. 44–61, 2014.
DOI: 10.1007/978-3-662-45079-6_4

even changes in the network more cost-effectively and faster. Indeed, simulation approaches can provide us with the possibility of comparing studies between new infrastructures designs or control algorithms without having to interfere in the real world.

Also, one important characteristic to bear in mind is that the domain of mobility (transportation of both vehicles and persons) presents an inherent complexity. It involves diverse heterogeneous entities either in structure or in behaviour, e.g. vehicles, pedestrians, traffic system, among others, which can interact, reflecting social behaviours that goes from coordination and collaboration to competition. Moreover, a high degree of uncertainty and dynamism especially when considering the urban context is uncovered.

To address the rising issues of these new trends a new generation of mobility systems emerged with the advent of what has been coined Intelligent Transportation Systems (ITSs), forcing architectures to become adaptable and accessible by different means so as to meet different requirements and a wide range of purposes. ITS arises as the synergy between the information and communication technologies (ICT) and the urban transportation systems, which include vehicles and networks that transport people and goods. The idea of such systems is to ensure the efficient utilisation of the available road capacity by controlling traffic operations and influencing drivers behaviour by providing proper information and stimuli.

The formalization of the ITS concept is to be considered a great achievement by the transportation engineering, practitioners and scientific communities. The explosion of the computing technology in terms of applications experimented in the last couple of decades brought together expertise from different scientific and technical disciplines giving birth to new computing and communication paradigms. A new type of systems coined as socio-technical arose from such mutual conjunctions where people and technology live in mutual symbiosis. The transportation and, generally speaking urban domain, could not be impermeable to such revolution. Indeed, it proves to be a valid field where new social and technological paradigms emerge. A new concept has been concocted to deal with this revolution, the so called future urban transportation (FUT) systems. The notion of mobility systems within FUT overcomes ITS limitations; instead of focusing only on the simple processes of transporting goods and persons they become self-conscious in terms of environment, accessibility, equality, security, and sustainability of resources [16]. People are placed as a central aspect, as well as are their preferences, of the urban systems, forcing architectures to become rather adaptable and accessible to their needs. Therefore, new technologies and methodologies are necessary to support these new models, which motivates this work.

Normally in the development of traffic solutions, the use of a simulator is very straightforward related to traffic flow and junction management. In spite of many attempts and published papers, the solutions presented do not make full use of the concept of intelligent agents. Additionally, the multi-agent systems

(MAS) metaphor has become recognized as a useful approach for modelling and simulating complex systems [14].

These new perspectives in urban mobility systems disclosed the need for the design of more human-centric and sustainable solutions. A framework that is capable of generating urban contexts (meaning a traffic network, infrastructures and the population of commuters) is definitely necessary so that analysts and designers can study, develop and evaluate their policies and strategies.

In this paper, we present a framework that meets all these requirements, providing practitioners and scientific communities with a tool that can instantiate an artificial society (AS) of heterogeneous drivers and intelligent traffic light management solutions, immersed in a realistic traffic environment. The concept of AS can be used by traffic managers or government institutions as a test-bed for the analysis of strategies and policies towards a social-aware and sustainable use of resources. Combining a powerful and standardized MAS development framework, JADE, with a large-scale microscopic traffic simulator, SUMO, allows different types of studies, namely intelligent traffic control algorithms, service design, additionally to studies for the evaluation of new policies and vehicle-to-vehicle (V2V) communication applications.

The remainder of the work is organized as follows. Section 2 motivates this research project and presents some related work, whereas Sect. 3 discusses on the tool-chain used to implement our proposed approach, detailed in Sect. 4. We illustrate our approach in Sect. 5 and draw conclusions in Sect. 6, identifying potential future work and further developments.

## 2   Related Work

Due to the high complexity and uncertainty of contemporary transportation systems, traditional traffic simulation fails to capture in detail all the dynamics that characterize them. For example, travelers can choose whether to travel or not, can change their planned itinerary at any moment, and their choices may be affected by any social, economic or environmental phenomena. Also, new performance measures brought about by an extensive future urban transport agenda and the implementation of the concept of smart cities pose additional requirements to which the user is central, not as easily integrated in traditional modelling approaches.

In order to appropriately represent, test, and analyse transportation control and management strategies, Fei-Yue Wang devised and introduced the concept of Artificial Transportation Systems (ATSs) [12,24]. Basically, ATS goes beyond traditional simulation methodologies and integrates the transportation system with other socio-economic urban systems with real-time information resulting in a powerful tool for transportation analysis, evaluation, decision-making and training. The foundations of ATS are to be searched on the paradigms of multi-agent systems, social simulation and artificial societies, as well as distributed computing, which provide adequate tools to represent interacting entities of complex domains such as intelligent transportation systems. Rossetti et al. [18]

provide a brief overview of contribution in ATS development along three dimensions: modelling issues and metaphors for ATS models, architectures for ATS, and practical applications of ATS. However, it results that very little has been advanced in what concerns the appropriate representation of users and their behaviour, in the various dimensions of Intelligent Transportation Systems.

Passos et al. [16] have carried out an evaluation of current available simulation environments and their ability to capture the aforementioned requirements. Their analysis features those characteristics of the future transportation systems where not only performance is essential but also the user entity is regarded as a key aspect playing an imperative whole in all social interactions taking place in such a complex domain. Among the desirable features that both works suggest is the agent-orientation of the candidate platform.

Although major traffic simulation packages and tools implement various important and advanced features, they still treat vehicles and drivers indistinctly following traditional modelling approaches such as car-following, lane changing and adopting a normative rather than a truly cognitive behavioural approach, reflecting users' decision-making and their preferences.

In the literature, some similar approaches can also be found that apply the agent metaphor to traffic simulation. ITSUMO [21] implements a cellular-automata approach and is formed up by four distinct modules, namely the data module, the simulation kernel, the driver definition module, and the visualization module. The agent metaphor is used in the sense it is possible to define driver decision-making procedures that simulate human-like cognition processes. The simulator also offer apropriate tools to test with intelligent traffic control strategies.

Balmer et al. [1] present the MATSim framework as a suitable tools for large-scale agent-based transportation simulations. In MATSim, each traveler of the real system is modeled as an individual agent and the simulator integrates activity-based demand generation with dynamic traffic assignment. The traffic dynamics is simulated using a macroscopic resolution of the transportation domain, whereas an activity-based demand approach models daily activities as diaries of trips for every "agent" in the population; each agent then performs journeys according to her own activity diary resulting in the network dynamics.

Within the Agentpolis project [10] it has been suggested a modular framework for the implementation, execution and analysis of simulation models of interaction-rich transport systems. The framework fully adopts the agent-based modelling paradigm, which makes it very versatile and capable of modelling systems with complex ad-hoc interactions and just-in-time decision-making.

Rossetti et al. [19], discusses an integrated multi-agent system that applies a methodological approach that allows for the assessment of today's intelligent transportation solutions through the metaphor of agents through a truly agent-directed simulation perspective. Their work conceptualizes the application domain in terms of agents and three basic subsystems are identified, namely the real world, the virtual domain, and the control strategies inductor that actually conducts the simulation process.

We believe however that it is possible to separate the drivers' decision-making and the vehicle control obtaining a clear separation of the supply (network) and demand (drivers choice) layers on the basis of the so-called delegated-agent idea. Following the MAS paradigm, drivers' decision-making process and choices will be embedded into a driver agent while the simulation platform implements the environment as well as the traffic infrastructure. This approach will allow planners to make a better design of the concepts envisaged by the new generation of urban transportation systems also under the perspective of the encompassed socio-technical aspects.

Similarly to our approach, ATSim [7] is presented as a multi-agent-based traffic simulation system to support global system throughput on a macro-level view, whereas individual vehicle decision-making is kept decentralized and separate from the traffic flow simulation itself. Thus, the infrastructure elements of the traffic domain, such as traffic lights and vehicles can make use of the agent paradigm with a reasonable performance. The system consists in coupling the commercial traffic simulation suite AimSun with the JADE platform for the development of multi-agent systems. In our approach however, we have opted to perform the traffic flow simulation using the open-source SUMO, instead of using a commercial simulator.

## 3   Tools

We propose a framework that allows us to build an artificial transportation system that represents all the entities composing it: a population of drivers feature deliberation abilities and situated in a road traffic environment. We face the problem of coupling two resolutions of the traffic system: one nanoscopic that reflects the decision-making module of a driver, and another microscopic traffic model reflecting vehicle interactions. It is obvious that we need to combine and synchronize different tools to achieve such multi-resolution setting.

The traffic simulation tool needs to implement the necessary concepts of the transportation domain (or to provide flexibility for additional implementation of them) and to provide a proper interface for controlling and monitoring the simulation entities and states. We will also need an intuitive MAS development framework, which will be used to implement the artificial society of drivers and various environment artifacts, such as the advanced traveler information systems (ATISs) and the intelligent control infrastructure.

In order to implement our requirements we opted for using the SUMO traffic simulator to represent the road network with the vehicle and the traffic control (physical) infrastructure. The JADE platform is used to represent the multi-agent systems composed of drivers (and generally speaking a synthetic population of travelers) and intelligent traffic management services (e.g. ATISs, intelligent traffic lights, and so forth). Finally, the TraSMAPI application is used to allow the synchronization between the agent-based population and SUMO.

## 3.1 SUMO/TraCI

A very popular tool to the traffic and transportation research community is the SUMO (Simulation of Urban MObility) traffic simulator. SUMO is a suite of applications that are used to design and implement realistic traffic simulations [11]. It represents both the road network infrastructure and the traffic demand and it has been used in several research problems such as route choice [8], traffic light algorithms [13], simulating vehicular communication [17], among others. The popularity of the simulation suite derives from the fact that it is open-source, highly portable, and offers microscopic and multi-modal traffic simulation packages designed to handle large road networks and to establish a common test-bed for implementing algorithms and models for traffic research. It is also stable and in continuous evolution supported by a large community of developers and users. Besides the aforementioned mentioned features it also facilitates interoperability with external applications in run time using TraCI (Traffic Control Interface), which allows developers to access a running road traffic simulation. TraCI uses a TCP-based client-server architecture providing access to SUMO. It opens a port in a SUMO simulation and waits for outbound well-defined commands, offering us with a wide range of features to use while the simulation is performed.

Nevertheless it still experience drawbacks from the traditional approach of dealing with vehicles and drivers indistinguishably. Although it can be extended due to its open-source nature, this obliges the user to directly implement patches to add any new functionality.

## 3.2 JADE

JADE (Java Agent DEvelopment Framework) [3] is a free software framework to develop agent-based applications. Its goal is to simplify the development of MAS while ensuring standard compliance through a comprehensive set of system services and agents. JADE is fully implemented in Java and is compliant with the Foundation for Intelligent Physical Agents (FIPA) specifications for interoperable multi-agent systems. Besides, this agent platform can be distributed across several machines, which do not even need to share the same Operating System (OS).

This framework can be considered a middleware that implements an agent platform and a development framework. It deals with all those aspects that are not peculiar to the agent internals and that are independent from the application domain, such as message transport, encoding and parsing, or the agent life-cycle. JADE's aim is to simplify the development of multi-agent systems while guaranteeing standard compliance with the FIPA specifications: naming service and yellow-page service comprising the Directory Facilitator (DF), message transport and parsing service, and a library of FIPA interaction protocols ready to be used. All agent communication is performed through message passing, where FIPA ACL is the language to represent messages. The agent platform can be dispersed on several computers, where each of which runs a single Java Virtual Machine (JVM). Each JVM is a container of agents that provides a complete run-time environment for agent execution and allows several agents to concurrently execute on the same host. Each agent is implemented as a single thread, however, agents often need to execute parallel tasks. As JAVA language offers multi-threading solutions, JADE also inherits these characteristics. Moreover it supports scheduling of cooperative behaviours, storing these tasks in a light and effective way. The runtime includes also some ready to use behaviours for the most common tasks in agent programming, such as FIPA interaction protocols [4]. Numerous R&D projects, where an interaction between several elements is required, and in which an autonomous and dynamic adaptation to complex relations is needed, have used JADE as a developing tool. In the traffic domain, there are several works that profit from the JADE platform for developing MAS-based traffic management solutions [20, 22].

### 3.3  TraSMAPI

TraSMAPI (Traffic Simulation Manager Application Programming Interface) is a synergy between two main components: an Application Programming Interface (API) and a Multi-Agent System framework. The API was built upon an abstraction level higher than most common microscopic traffic simulators so that, ideally, the solution should be independent from the microscopic simulator coice. This is guaranteed as far as the chosen simulators allow it, and provided that their communication interface differs and they do not implement the same set of functions. This feature allows the comparison of results from different simulators using exactly the same implemented traffic management solution.

The multi-agent system framework is a module that is meant to serve as a starting point for the creation of multi-agent systems. It allows the creation of new agents by following a common interface. The agents are created with a reference to one or multiple objects in the simulation gaining direct access to its artifacts or entities. As far as our work is concerned, we aim to replace that MAS framework module with more widely distributed MAS frameworks, such as JADE. This approach allows us to use TraSMAPI also in the implementation of real-world solutions since it will have a more mature, generic and FIPA-compliant MAS development framework.

## 4  Research Method

We propose a layered approach to represent drivers' decision-making capabilities within the framework, which are: a strategic layer that encompasses cognitive functions and decision-making processes, and a tactical layer where the basic control of the vehicle resides. In fact, with the previous division, we were able to decouple driver's cognition from her behaviour (seen as demand) from the traffic simulation that represents only the physical infrastructures (seen as supply).

We want to have agent-based ITS solutions implemented in JADE and operated in the SUMO environment. The path to accomplish so is to have an heterogeneous artificial society of drivers in the JADE agent platform whilst each of these agents is responsible for one vehicle in the SUMO's traffic environment.

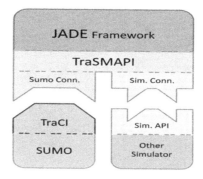

**Fig. 1.** Framework architecture

## 4.1 Integration

Taking into consideration all the general requirements and goals we have devised the following architecture as depicted in Fig. 1. We can observe the main contribution of TraSMAPI in our framework.

TraSMAPI provides an abstraction over different possible microscopic simulators, which makes our platform completely independent from the simulator used. Besides, it makes possible further studies on simulation results comparisons, since it is possible to test the same solution, i.e. source code, in various simulators, hence demonstrating TraSMAPI's transparency and self-reliance. In addition to the TraSMAPI block, we can also observe that JADE is directly connected to the microscopic traffic API (TraSMAPI), which has a communication model for the SUMO Simulator that reflects the basic API for the interaction with the simulator.

The microscopic traffic simulator offers an API for access to its simulation state - TraCI. For an external application to communicate with this software it must obey the TraCI communication protocol and messages types. The SUMO Communication Module attached to TraSMAPI converts this low-level simulator API to a higher-level programmer's perspective, which will be then used by our artificial society of drivers implemented in JADEs MAS development framework coupled to TraSMAPI.

## 4.2 Driver Agent Architecture

To build and associate each driver agent with a simulated vehicle and endorse her with all driving decisions, skills and cognitive characteristics would be computationally very expensive. To simulate hundreds or thousands of vehicles and drivers' decision-making in JADE we have adopted the delegate-agent concept, which has been used in [23], to separate the tactical from the strategic layer of the agent, and execute them in parallel, thus improving performance (see Fig. 2).

The idea of separating the tactical from the strategic layer of a driver agent is based on the different time-scale and complexity of the cognitive and reactive

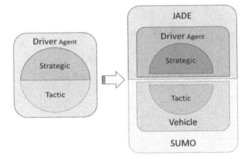

**Fig. 2.** Driver's Layers: tactic-reactive in SUMO; strategic-cognitive layer in JADE.

actions related to the primary task of driving. That is, the driver will need a short time to take an action reacting to a traffic event such as accelerating, slowing down, changing lane, or over taking. On the other hand the task of collecting and processing information related to traffic messages or other recommendation necessitates longer time periods. The tactic-reactive layer, following a rule-based behaviour, was entrusted to the microscopic traffic simulator, taking care of reactive actions associated with driving itself. Thus, drivers endow the feature expressed by SUMO's driver behaviour model, as follows:

- accelerating and breaking actions
- lane-changing behaviour
- anticipating events

The strategic layer, expressed as the route-choice or adaptive learning behaviour, was kept in JADE framework. Here, the researcher can implement her own strategic architecture, from pure reactive to pure cognitive agent architectures. Following are possible high-level reasoning tasks the agent can perform:

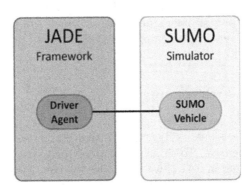

**Fig. 3.** Vehicle abstraction through the architectural design.

- information assimilation
- mental map and representation of the network
- reaction to traffic messages

In order to achieve these ideas, we need to extend the scope of TrasMAPI, enabling it to build an abstraction over the vehicle entity, as illustrated in Fig. 3. We have implemented the communication protocol regarding the methods of a vehicle for variable retrieval or state change taking into account the compliance with the well-defined instructions of TraCI, for further information see TraCI's documentation and reference [25], where the protocol and message flow are presented and detailed.

## 4.3    ATIS Artifacts Implementation

The concept of the artifact according to activity theory is to enable action and mediate interactions of the active components in an environment. So, artifacts mediate the interaction among agents, as well as between agents and their environment. On the other hand, artifacts embody the part of the environment that can be designed and controlled to support participants activities [15]. Since artifacts affect the space of agent interaction coordination, cooperation and competition issues can arise. One can easily see how artifacts possibly play a key role in engineering self-organizing systems, as they can be noticed in the traffic domain (such as coordination among drivers for platooning formations, or between adjacent traffic lights to allow green-wave coordination).

By using the agent concept as a programming paradigm to build and model ATIS artifacts we are able to blend them into JADE. The purpose of ATIS is to acquire, process and present information to travelers assisting them in their travel activities. Thus ATIS artifacts can operate as amplifier of the observable space of the driver agent by "extending" its spatial cognition. The agent processes the information and eventually changes her plans according to the input reducing this way travel time. ATIS also facilitates the communication among driver agents as it can receive notifications of events in the network (SUMO environment) and broadcast it back to the whole network. Thus, we can consider this infrastructure as a receiver and a service provider, as we observe in Fig. 4.

The sources, from which the ATIS infrastructures gather information are quite vast. They vary from network data, simulation information and accident notification by drivers, building a common knowledge base on traffic information that can be abstracted as a blackboard. An ATIS agent is responsible for a certain type of work and field of action. We have defined three types of ATIS Agents, the Radio Broadcast (RB), the Variable Message Sign (VMS), and the Informative Traffic Lights (ITL), as seen in Fig. 5. Each ATIS entity uses the microscopic traffic simulator SUMO as a sensory environment. To represent this infrastructure inside the simulator we used the SUMO's Polygon4 abstraction, which does not have an active role in the simulation though. To gather this sensory data APIs calls must be invoked. However, the mere fact of asking a

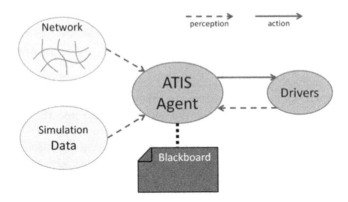

**Fig. 4.** ATIS interaction with environment and drivers

**Fig. 5.** All three implemented ATIS entities

variable and getting its value can be quite time consuming, since it demands the exchange of two messages, i.e. the request and reading the variable value. Considering this performance issue, SUMO's TraCI provides two subscription commands that showed to be very useful to retrieve information on network data: variable subscription and context subscription. With these commands, one can register a request for value retrieval for a defined amount of time, which eliminates the request phase, thus reducing the execution time in about half of the original time.

Variable subscriptions provide a periodical update on a structure variable. Context subscriptions allow to obtain specific values from surrounding objects of a certain object within a defined range. This is the reason why we have represented the ATIS entity as a polygon object in the simulated environment. With this implementation we were able to create an entity that gathers facts from the network and simulation data, and provides them to the driver agents through JADEs messaging network.

## 5   Scenario Illustration

To illustrate the capabilities of the platform we will consider two scenarios where drivers need to make choices over possible routes to follow. The first example shows how agent can decide on-line the fastest route to choose between an origin and destination. The second example is related to the *Braess Paradox*. Here a

**Fig. 6.** Eichstätt transportation network

synthetic population of drivers adapt by learning their daily routes following a day-to-day (individual) traffic flow analysis.

### 5.1 Route Choice Example

As a first scenario we have used and improved the network model of the German city of Eichstätt, using the JOSM application to correct some intersections and lane cardinality (see Fig. 6). Graphically we added the Google Maps decals to improve the user immersion during simulation visualization. The configuration files used to load SUMO simulation are only the network file and GUI settings. In this experimental set-up we intend to reproduce the drivers' decision-making process in route choice based on previous travel times.

With our framework we can instantiate a Driver to each vehicle simulated in SUMO. Therefore one may use all the methods which this simulated instance has, such as change destination, speed, route, among others. In the beginning of the simulation it is given to each entity of the AS a random origin edge and orientation and a different random destination. With this, the agents' reactive layer in SUMO can make use of its shortest path algorithms and calculate the best route based on travel time to accomplish each driver's desire.

As a proof of concept, each Driver sets a value to its travel time table in SUMO, so that when the reroute-by-travel-time algorithm is called, it will take into account the updated values in the table. This approach argues in favour of the drivers' awareness and decision-making capabilities. The instantiated traffic-light entities are an extension of a previous experience concerning advisory-based traffic control [13].

### 5.2 Braess' Paradox Illustration

There are generally two types of travel behaviour: user-optimizing behaviour, in which travelers select their optimal route, and are generally characterized as "selfish"; and system-optimizing behaviour, in which a central controller directs traffic. Our work focuses on the former and thus the Braess' paradox occurs only for user-optimizing behaviours.

In an urban area with a lot of traffic, adding a new road to distribute and facilitate traffic may seem an intuitive idea. However, according to the Braess' paradox, just the opposite occurs: a new route added in a transportation network actually increases the travel time of all individual travelers [5,6]. The Braess' Paradox is a good illustration of how easily our intuition about collective interaction can be fooled.

Car drivers seek to minimise the time to get from origin O to destination D. However, car drivers may not be able to act independently of each other: collective interactions may influence individual behaviour. We have made this as a proof-of-concept experimentation scenario of one of the numerous uses that this platform provides to the community of researchers and practitioners. In this case we tried to replicate the Braess' paradox by setting up an artificial society of "selfish" learning drivers, in a well-defined scenario. Their goal is to get from point A to point B the fastest way possible.

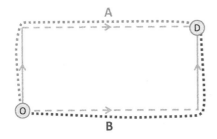
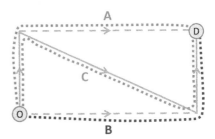

**Fig. 7.** Two route network          **Fig. 8.** Three route network

The network, sketched in Fig. 7, is an abstraction of a network being composed by two symmetrical routes, each of which consists of a fast section and a slow one. Then at a certain time, a new fastest road is added (Fig. 8) providing drivers more and better road resources. We have built an artificial society of Q-learning drivers, which will "live" for 500 days and perform, each day, a trip from point O to D. When arrived at destination, each driver registers her travel time (TT):

$$TT = arrivalTime - departureTime \tag{1}$$

Taking the environment into account we have modelled it in a finite-state automaton, with 3 edges from node 'O' to node 'D', and we have built the correspondent Q-table to each of the driver agents, where each route choice in state $s$ generates a *utility*.

Since our problem is scalar, depending only on the route choice and not also on the current state, we can simplify it to $Q(r)$, being $r$ the route chosen. Hence our utility-function is:

$$Q(r) = (1 - \eta) Q(r) + \eta.R \tag{2}$$

being $\eta$ the learning rate and $R$ the Reward function:

$$R = \frac{aTT}{TT} - 1 \tag{3}$$

whilst $TT$ is current travel time and $aTT$ is the average travel time of all trips:

$$aTT = \frac{\sum TT}{\sharp trips} \tag{4}$$

For our test-bed we have defined an exploration and an exploitation time in each network configuration for all 500 days. Each network configuration, meaning different route arrangement, is **explored** by the driver agents during 50 days, in which the drivers are randomly assigned a route so as to retrieve knowledge from its journey time, thus updating her Q-table. The remaining days are **exploited** by the driver according to their utility values. Drivers' departure time is equally distributed along the first hour of the day. So in the two-route scenario the drivers will perform 50 days of exploration and 150 days of exploitation. Afterwards, they will have another 50 days of exploration and 250 days for exploiting their best options.

We have performed several tests with various numbers of drivers to observe their learning process in a route-choice setting and we identified two different patterns. Following, two different setups of traffic density have been considered. First we run the simulation with a very low vehicle density that did not put in evidence the paradox scenario. Because the departure times of the drivers were very temporally sparse the new route has not been jammed and therefore chosen by the majority of the drivers. On the second setup we have explored a scenario with a high density of vehicles, approximately one vehicle each two seconds. In this case, we have noticed the increase in travel times and the **underutiliza-tion** of the additional route, regardless of being the fastest alternative. This experiment is plotted in Fig. 9.

In the first **exploitation** phase [50,200], the number of vehicles that chose route A or route B is nearly the same, without fluctuations, which establishes a constant average travel time (observed in the bottom graph). During the second **exploration** phase [200,250], we verify that the average travel time in the new route C is a bit shorter. Hence, in the beginning of the second **exploitation** period [250,500] the drivers should have a great utility in the choice of C. In fact, we can observe that almost every 1900 vehicles chose to travel through it i.e. route C, **overpassing the initial average travel time**, recorded when there were only 2 routes available. With this insertion, the average travel time increased from approximately 1000 s to a staggering 3000 s.

The learning drivers, encountering such a scenario, quickly changed their option based on the utility of route C. They returned to their previous choice avoiding the overpopulated route improving their travel time. We can observe this event in the quick variation of peaks in the upper plot in just approximately 20 days. With this learning process the overall travel time drops as well as the **underutilization** of route C, which becomes the less used route, regardless being the fastest one.

However, the purpose of the paper is not to discuss the Braess' Paradox, as it has already been done by Bazzan and Klügl [2] but to illustrate how the tool can be used in a realistic case study, using a microscopic traffic simulator

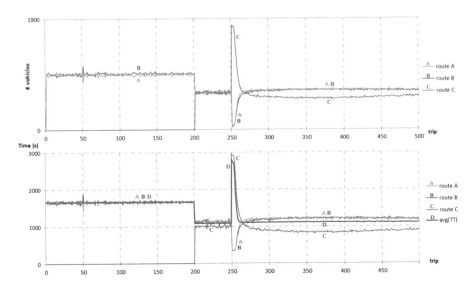

**Fig. 9.** Occupation and travel time in the 1900 vehicle test. Top: Occupation(trip); Bottom: Travel-Time(trip)

and an artificial society of adaptive drivers. The adaptation by learning aims to represent knowledge acquisition and exploitation of a network.

## 6  Conclusion and Future Work

Traffic systems have been subjected to a lot of improvement in the last decades and travelers have, in general, witnessed a revolution in the way a trip is planned in urban networks. Hence, facing the current traffic situation in most developed countries it is now imperative to foster new transportation methods using state-of-the-art technologies towards Future Urban Transport (FUT).

Simulation has proved to be an effective approach to analysing and designing novel traffic solutions in socio-technical systems. We have devised a conceptual architecture of an artificial transportation system based on a well-established platform for the development of multi-agent systems and a popular open-source microscopic traffic simulator. Following the concept of delegated agents we define and implement a two-layered architecture representing an driver agent where we differentiate between the reactive and cognitive capabilities of the agent. To illustrate the potentiality of our approach in representing human behaviour, we built a synthetic population of adaptive drivers, where we experimented the knowledge representation of the network using Reinforcement Learning techniques. Finally, we have shown how the proposed framework can be used to instantiate MAS of different nature over the traffic domain complying fully with the notion of the socio-technical systems and other embedded intelligent artifacts (e.g. ATIS, intelligent traffic control, and so forth).

With respect to microscopic traffic simulators and specifically to SUMO, we extend their capabilities as we can allow the design of truly AI-based solution to be tested in the traffic domain without the necessity of modifying the core of the simulator. Also we have extended the type of possible analysis one can perform. The notion of the 2-layered architecture allows the simulator to "implement" memory and thus we can improve the within-to-day and day-to-day traffic flow analysis considering cognitive and behavioural aspects of the driver based on her own preferences.

Generally speaking the proposed tool also reveals great flexibility for multi-agent systems design and development in the traffic and transportation domains. Developers can easily model and test their own artificial society of drivers, where each agents is presented with her own preferences and beliefs. Such artificial society can thus be used to design solutions based on individual or collective intelligence and participation (social-awareness) or as a test-bed for policy evaluation by governmental institutions and decision-makers. This approach will help practitioners to design and test more human-centric, cost-efficient and environmental sustainable solutions. As future developments, not only vehicle-to-X (V2X) scenarios but also the development of new policies and incentive mechanisms studies might be carried out and evaluated through our platform.

**Acknowledgements.** This project has been partially supported by FCT (Fundação para a Ciência e a Tecnologia), the Portuguese Agency for R&D, under grant SFRH/BD/67202/2009.

# References

1. Balmer, M., Rieser, M., Meister, K., Charypar, D., Lefebvre, N., Nagel, K., Axhausen, K.: Matsim-t: Architecture and simulation times. In: Multi-Agent Systems for Traffic and Transportation Engineering, pp. 57–78 (2009)
2. Bazzan, A.L.C., Klügl, F.: Case studies on the braess paradox: Simulating route recommendation and learning in abstract and microscopic models. Trans. Res. C **13**(4), 299–313 (2005)
3. Bellifemine, F., Caire, G., Poggi, A., Rimassa, G.: JADE-A White Paper, Sept. 2003. Online document accessible under. http://jade.tilab.com/papers/2003/WhitePaperJADEEXP.pdf (2003). Accessed on 22 March 2008
4. Bellifemine, F., Poggi, A., Rimassa, G.: JADEA FIPA-compliant agent framework. In: Proceedings of PAAM, vol. 99, p. 33. London (1999)
5. Braess, D.: Über ein Paradoxon aus der Verkehrsplanung. Math. Methods Oper. Res. **12**(1), 258–268 (1968)
6. Braess, D., Nagurney, A., Wakolbinger, T.: On a paradox of traffic planning. Transp. Sci. **39**(4), 446–450 (2005)
7. Chu, V.H., Görmer, J., Müller, J.P.: Atsim: Combining aimsum and jade for agent-based traffic simulation. Avances en inteligencia artificial. Actas de CAEPIA11 1 (2011)
8. Doering, M., Pögel, T., Wolf, L.: Dtn routing in urban public transport systems. In: Proceedings of the 5th ACM Workshop on Challenged Networks, CHANTS '10, pp. 55–62. ACM, New York (2010). http://doi.acm.org/10.1145/1859934.1859947

9. Doytsher, Y., Kelly, P., Khouri, R., McLAREN, R., Potsiou, C.: Rapid urbanization and mega cities: The need for spatial information management. Research study by FIG Commission 3. FIG Publication No 48 (2010)

10. Jakob, M., Moler, Z.: Modular framework for simulation modelling of interaction-rich transport systems. In: Proceedings of the 16th IEEE Intelligent Transportation Systems Conference (ITSC 2013) (2013)

11. Krajzewicz, D., Erdmann, J., Behrisch, M., Bieker, L.: Recent development and applications of SUMO - Simulation of Urban MObility. Int. J. Adv. Syst. Meas. 5(3&4), 128–138 (2012)

12. Li, J., Tang, S., Wang, X., Wang, F.Y.: A software architecture for artificial transportation systems - principles and framework (2007)

13. Macedo, J., Soares, M., Timóteo, I., Rossetti, R.J.: An approach to advisory-based traffic control. In: 2012 7th Iberian Conference on Information Systems and Technologies (CISTI), pp. 1–6. IEEE (2012)

14. Moya, L.J., Tolk, A.: Towards a taxonomy of agents and multi-agent systems. In: Proceedings of the 2007 Spring Simulation Multiconference, vol. 2, pp. 11–18. SpringSim '07, Society for Computer Simulation International, San Diego, CA, USA (2007)

15. Omicini, A., Ricci, A., Viroli, M.: Artifacts in the A&A meta-model for multi-agent systems. Auton. Agents Multi-Agent Syst. 17(3), 432–456 (2008)

16. Passos, L.S., Rossetti, R.J.F., Kokkinogenis, Z.: Towards the next-generation traffic simulation tools: a first appraisal. In: 2011 6th Iberian Conference on Information Systems and Technologies (CISTI), pp. 1–6 (2011)

17. Rieck, D., Schünemann, B., Radusch, I., Meinel, C.: Efficient traffic simulator coupling in a distributed v2x simulation environment. In: Proceedings of the 3rd International ICST Conference on Simulation Tools and Techniques, pp. 72:1–72:9. SIMUTools '10, ICST (Institute for Computer Sciences, Social-Informatics and Telecommunications Engineering), ICST, Brussels, Belgium, Belgium (2010). http://dx.doi.org/10.4108/ICST.SIMUTOOLS2010.8640

18. Rossetti, R.J.F., Liu, R., Tang, S.: Guest editorial special issue on artificial transportation systems and simulation. IEEE Trans. Intell. Transp. Syst. 12(2), 309–312 (2011)

19. Rossetti, R.J., Oliveira, E.C., Bazzan, A.L.: Towards a specification of a framework for sustainable transportation analysis. In: 13th Portuguese Conference on Artificial Intelligence. Citeseer, Guimarães (2007)

20. Sanchez Passos, L., Rossetti, R.: Traffic light control using reactive agents. In: 2010 5th Iberian Conference on Information Systems and Technologies (CISTI), pp. 1–6. IEEE (2010)

21. Castro da Silva, B., Bazzan, A.L.C., Andriotti, G.K., Lopes, F., de Oliveira, D.: ITSUMO: An intelligent transportation system for urban mobility. In: Böhme, T., Larios Rosillo, V.M., Unger, H., Unger, H. (eds.) IICS 2004. LNCS, vol. 3473, pp. 224–235. Springer, Heidelberg (2006)

22. Van den Bosch, A.T., Menken, M.R., van Breukelen, M., van Katwijk, R.T.: A test bed for multi-agent systems and road traffic management. In: Proceedings of the 15th Belgian-Netherlands Conference on Artificial Intelligence (BNAIC'03), pp. 43–50 (2003)

23. Wahle, J., Bazzan, A.L.C., Klügl, F., Schreckenberg, M.: The impact of real-time information in a two-route scenario using agent-based simulation. Transp. Res. Part C: Emer.Technol. 10(56), 399–417 (2002)

24. Wang, F.Y.: Integrated intelligent control and management for urban traffic systems. In: Intelligent Transportation Systems, 2003, Proceedings, vol. 2, pp. 1313–1317. IEEE (2003)
25. Wegener, A., Piórkowski, M., Raya, M., Hellbrück, H., Fischer, S., Hubaux, J.P.: TraCI: An interface for coupling road traffic and network simulators. In: Proceedings of the 11th communications and networking simulation symposium, CNS '08, pp. 155–163. ACM, New York (2008). http://doi.acm.org/10.1145/1400713.1400740

# Sumo as a Service – Building up a Web Service to Interact with SUMO

Mario Krumnow[⊠]

Chair of Traffic Control Systems and Process Automation,
Dresden University of Technology, Andreas-Schubert-Str. 23,
01069 Dresden, Germany
mario.krumnow@tu-dresden.de

**Abstract.** To interact with a simulation at runtime is often demanded within the scope of research studies. Therefore the microscopic traffic simulation software SUMO has a real-time I/O data interface (TraCI). This interface offers the possibility for a bidirectional communication between the user application and the simulation. Only few software implementations can handle that protocol, one of them is the Python TraCI Client being included into the simulation suite. Though depending on the preferred programming language, a specific implementation is needed. A solution designed to cover the problem is a standardized protocol interacting with SUMO, like the simple object access protocol (SOAP). This protocol can easily be integrated into a lot of programming languages, and is implemented as part of a Web service. This solution offers a lot of opportunities e.g. an unlimited number of clients.

**Keywords:** Microscopic traffic simulation · Web service · SOAP · WSDL

## 1 Motivation

The main reason for building a Web service is to make the communication with the Traffic Control Interface more comfortable, even for people who are not familiar with Python.

Due to a clear and user-friendly communication the SUMO user will be able to focus on the analysis of traffic and transportation data [1]. Furthermore the Web service is platform-independent, which permits the user to utilize various kinds of programming languages. The Web service handles multiple connections simultaneously. This is a base requirement for using the micro simulation as a service in the field of traffic management centers [2, 7, 8]. Therefore it makes no difference where the application is located or which programming language has been used to interact with the simulation.

## 2 Implementation of the Web Service

### 2.1 Integration of TraCI

As a first implementation the programming language Java has been used to interact with SUMO. Java is platform independent and very robust due to the embedded

© Springer-Verlag Berlin Heidelberg 2014
M. Behrisch et al. (Eds.): SUMO 2013, LNCS 8594, pp. 62–70, 2014.
DOI: 10.1007/978-3-662-45079-6_5

Exception Handling concept. A project named traci4j already implements a TraCI Handler that generates Byte Messages for the requests and responses for Java [9]. So these parts of the code provide the base for a new Web service which is now called TraaS (TraCI as a service).

In traci4j only a couple of functions of the TraCI API has been implemented which show the main functionality of the written code. In order to offer as much functions as possible the software needs to be extended. Due to the fact that the web service will not support streaming the subscription feature is not available.

To get an overview about all TraCI methods which are available a special software tool has been developed. That program reads and interprets the python code of the TraCI client which is up to date. The source code is located in the default installation package of SUMO. All recognized functions as well as the available comments have been extracted and stored in a single XML File.

By then a determination in getter and setter methods has already been done. This means the functions have been marked with a couple of XML attributes. That import process is semi-automated due to the fact that the original Python source code does not yet follow a standardized schema.

In order to support this task a basic java software tool has been developed, which has the facility to show and edit the information of the XML within a graphical user interface (GUI). This tool uses the external library dom4j [10] for the XML parsing and JavaFX for the GUI part (Fig. 1).

After validating and editing the XML file over 250 methods have been named and described. The data type for each input argument and the returning values has been defined.

Subsequently another java program generates the required java classes by processing the XML file. This is an important part because files for the TraCI client as well as for the Java Web service are being created at the same time.

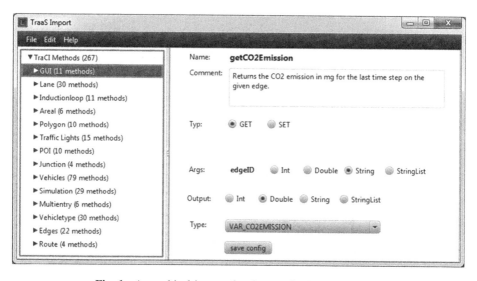

**Fig. 1.** A graphical java tool to import the TraCI functions

To work as a Web service every value has to be serializable to be embedded in a SOAP Message. This is no problem with primitive data types like double or integer which are working by default. For other data types like the SUMO StringList or the compound structure elements some new Java classes has been generated. As a result the class SumoStringlist is an implementation of the Java List Object which is part of the java collection framework. Some more classes have been generated in order to represent all necessary values of the appropriate compounds within the Python code.

The Java classes have the same function names as those used in the original Python code. Additionally the order of the arguments has been preserved. Usually Java methods can be distinguished into two types: on the one hand the getter methods with a returning value and on the other hand setter methods without any returning value. All that TraCI functions have been dedicated in one of those two issues.

In both cases the TraCI request message is constructed by a class called Sumo-Command. Depending on the occurrence of a returning value the method is a getter or setter method.

For every command block an extra class has been generated. As a result there are at least thirteen different classes (Fig. 1).

It has been necessary to change several parts of the original traci4j code to support all these new data types. Furthermore some unnecessary parts were removed to simplify the application. At the end of that process the developed software does not have any external references like log4j or similar dependencies.

The way the TraCI functions are imported is going to be improved in the future e.g. instead of the python client the original source code of the C++ TraCI Server API should be used. Moreover Test cases should be generated by default within the importing process. To take account on changes in the functionally of the TraCI Code in SUMO there should be some scripts which checks the java client in cases of changes.

## 2.2    Building the Web Service

To work as a Web service some java classes need to be added to offer the endpoint communication. This means that the service binds on a specific IP address and on a

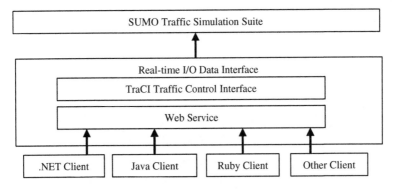

**Fig. 2.** Concept of the Web service

specific port. Consequently it is possible to have multiple Web server instances on a single server by using different ports. In Fig. 2 the concept of the Web service is shown.

To offer all the methods of the java TraCI client to the Web service another java class has been generated by the help of a small script. All the public web methods have been marked with a special annotation. This is necessary to make the methods visible and also available for the Web service client. For each method a prefix has been added to ease distinguishing between different command block functions by origin. Every method belonging to a vehicle, gets the prefix "Vehicle_". For example the method for changing the lane of a vehicle is named Vehicle_changeLane(arg1, arg2).

By using the SOAP protocol the communication is based on XML messages, so the whole request and the response messages are encoded in XML. The used bandwidth is much higher than the TraCI Byte communication because of the large overhead of XML. In Fig. 3 an example of such an XML response message for a lane shape request is shown.

The relatively huge bandwidth caused by the SOAP messages is a disadvantage of this concept. However considering that the bandwidth will not be the bottle neck in times of gigabit Ethernet networks this approach is sufficient. A comparison between the TraCI Byte code communication and the corresponding SOAP communication would be interesting, especially regarding to the emerging latency times.

```xml
<?xml version="1.0"?>
<S:Envelope xmlns:S="http://schemas.xmlsoap.org/soap/envelope/">
    <S:Body>
        <ns2:Lane_getShapeResponse xmlns:ns2="http://ws.tudresden.de/">
            <return>
                <coords>
                    <x>160.68</x>
                    <y>50.17</y>
                </coords>
                <coords>
                    <x>52.89</x>
                    <y>49.34</y>
                </coords>
            </return>
        </ns2:Lane_getShapeResponse>
    </S:Body>
</S:Envelope>
```

**Fig. 3.** SOAP message for a shape response

## 2.3    Performance of the Web Service

In a first research a comparison has been made between the runtime using the original Python API and the TraaS Application. It is possible to use TraaS as a Java library, which can easily be integrated into a user Java application. In that case the main task of the library is encoding and decoding the TraCI Byte messages. This is equivalent to the SUMO Python Client. High loads of TCP/IP network packages will not appear. While running TraaS as a standalone Web service, the application handles all client connections. Moreover the encoding and decoding of the SOAP messages has to be done. Obviously the runtime increases because of the additional XML handling being used by the SOAP protocol.

Three different ways have been compared to interact with SUMO. Therefore a standard simulation case, inserting vehicles and increasing the simulation time has been chosen. In that case road with 2 lanes and a distance of 10 km were modelled (Fig. 4). In that network there are no intersection or traffic lights which increases the simulation time.

**Fig. 4.** Simulation for the benchmark

Firstly a Python Client has been written using the defaults Python API (Fig. 5). Secondly *TraaS* has been applied as a referenced library for a user Java application (Fig. 6). Thirdly a Java application, using *TraaS* as a standalone Web service has been built. The last one is quite similar to the code snippet shown in Fig. 5. The command line options have been equal for the three examples.

```
for i in range(duration):
    traci.simulationStep()
    traci.vehicle.add('v'+str(i), 'route', 0, 0, 13.8, 0, 'car')
```

**Fig. 5.** Python example for the benchmark

```
for(int i=0; i<duration; i++){
    conn.do_timestep(1);
    conn.do_job_set(Vehicle.add("v"+i, "car", "route", 0, 0, 13.8, 0));
}
```

**Fig. 6.** Java example for the benchmark

The 64 BIT version of the SUMO application has been used for that benchmark. The applications have been executed on an Intel® Core i3 Processor with an amount of 4 GB of physical RAM available. Each simulation were run at least ten times to build a average value for the runtime. By variation of the duration value the results in Table 1 have been reached. The assumption that the runtime increases by using the Web service has been assured. This is important especially for simulations with small networks and a small traffic volume because the simulation takes significantly more time. In huge simulation scenarios the runtime of SUMO itself dominates the overall runtime. The time for communication is negligible short. To verify this assumption some more benchmarks need to be built.

**Table 1.** Comparison of the different runtimes of the different applications

| Duration | Python code | TraaS as library | TraaS as Web service |
|----------|-------------|------------------|----------------------|
| 500      | 829 ms      | 1133 ms          | 4514 ms              |
| 1000     | 1409 ms     | 1689 ms          | 8177 ms              |
| 2000     | 2397 ms     | 2786 ms          | 15455 ms             |
| 5000     | 5384 ms     | 6333 ms          | 38049 ms             |
| 10000    | 11627 ms    | 13678 ms         | 76531 ms             |

## 3  Using the Web Service

The Web service implements a start function ensuring SUMO to be launched with a defined configuration file and listening on a specified port. Furthermore the different clients are able to connect to the Web service and have access to all of the getter and setter methods. For real time simulations a timer application is required, which does a simulation step. Building up new clients is a straight forward process because ready-made tools like the wsimport binary in Java. The build-in tools in MS Visual Studio for the .NET programming languages are used to integrate the Web service. The integration in Visual Studio is shown in Fig. 7.

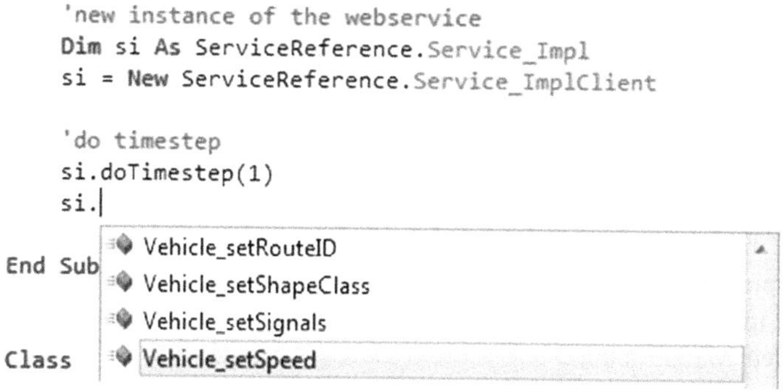

```
'new instance of the webservice
Dim si As ServiceReference.Service_Impl
si = New ServiceReference.Service_ImplClient

'do timestep
si.doTimestep(1)
si.|
End Sub    Vehicle_setRouteID
           Vehicle_setShapeClass
           Vehicle_setSignals
Class      Vehicle_setSpeed
```

**Fig. 7.** Example of a VB.NET application

The Web service has already been used successfully by students and research engineers at Dresden University of Technology. Various scientific studies have shown the practical significance of the Web service and have helped to develop and improve its features [3–5].

An example of a student research project [6] is shown in Fig. 8. This work used *TraaS* as a library in order to interact with SUMO. A user-defined library has been used in front of the Web service to handle some default tasks, like the import and export of different data sources. A graphical user interface named SumoInteractive has been developed in Java. It offers the possibility to manipulate some vehicles in the simulation. By changing the values of some sliders the related parameters of the simulation are affected directly.

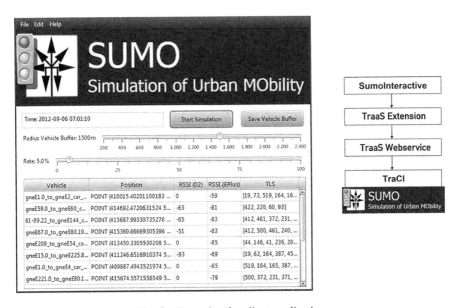

**Fig. 8.**  Example of a client application

Another work implements the *TraaS* Library into Mathworks® Matlab which is very comfortable because of the java language support which is built in Matlab. The *TraaS* methods become available as basic toolbox functions, which can be easily integrated by drag and drop into the user project [12].

Consequently more detailed models of single vehicles become available. The accurate behavior of vehicles does not only depend on the car following model and the change lane model. In addition the specific attributes of a chosen engine can influence the target trajectories. Matlab is used for computing the corresponding gear and revolutions per minute. Hence the vehicles in the simulation adapt their velocity based on that computed Matlab model.

In the near future the Matlab Toolboxes should be generated automatically during the import process to have all the TraCI functions available in Matlab as well.

## 4   Conclusions

The use of a Web service in order to communicate with SUMO is very beneficial especially for educational purposes. Users can freely choose their preferred programming language and interact with the traffic simulation immediately. *TraaS* provides simple access to SUMO especially for users who are not familiar with Python. The benefit of ta existing library which handles all the communication with SUMO becomes available for every programming language which support SOAP.

Obviously the runtime of TraCI commands is more time consuming using the Web service because of the connection handling and the necessary XML parsing tasks. However this additional time is of less consequence in large simulation, because the runtime is determined mainly by the traffic volume and the dynamic processes like variable message signs or traffic lights. Nevertheless it is useful to run *TraaS* as java library when it is possible to avoid the extra computation time for the SOAP communication.

A final target could be the integration of the Web service directly into the SUMO source code. With some new command line options the web service should be configured and activated. So the TraCI interface becomes more popular to the public because of the easy to use data protocol. New methods of the TraCI server becomes visible in the moment they are implemented not in the moment the TraCI client is extended.

Since summer 2013 the project TraaS is available under a General Public License (GPL) and is hosted at SourceForge [11]. Since release 0.19.0 the source code is also available in the contributed section of SUMO.

# References

1. SUMO – Simulation of Urban Mobility (2012). Institute of Transportation Systems, German Aerospace Center, Germany. http://sumo.sf.net. Accessed 11 August 2013
2. Microscopic real-time simulation of Dresden using data from the traffic management system VAMOS, Proceedings of the 19th ITS World Congress Vienna, Austria, 25 October 2012
3. Schaltzeitprognose verkehrsadaptiver Lichtsignalanlagen im Rahmen des Projektes EFA 2014/ 2, Mario Krumnow, VIMOS, 29 November 2012
4. Arlt, A.: Realitätsnahe Simulation des Verkehrsflusses auf der Süd-West-Umfahrung in Dresden mit SUMO unter Berücksichtigung des MIV und des ÖPNV (in German). Report student research project, Dresden University of Technology, Germany (2012)
5. Reiche, M.: Vorher-Nachher-Analyse der Emissionsbelastung am Knotenpunkt Nürnberger Platz im Rahmen der ÖPNV-Bevorrechtigung des NSV-Projektes (in German). Report student research project, Dresden University of Technology, Germany (2012)
6. Wießner, E: Analyse der Datenmengen der Car-2-Infrastructure Kommunikation realitätsnahe Simulation unterschiedlicher Testszenarien (in German). Report student research project, Dresden University of Technology, Germany (2013)
7. Krimmling, J., Franke, R., Engelmann, R., Körner, M.: Erfahrungen mit dem vollautomatischen baulastträgerübergreifenden Betrieb der Dynamischen Wegweisungskomponente im Operativen Straßenverkehrsmanagementsystem VAMOS (in German). In: Proceedings HEUREKA 2011 – Optimierung in Verkehr und Transport, Forschungsgesellschaft für Straßen- und Verkehrswesen .e.V., Cologne, Germany (2011)
8. Krumnow, M: Verkehrsmikrosimulationen mit Echtzeitdaten – Herausforderungen und Chancen, 9. VIMOS Tagung, Dresden
9. http://traci4j.sourceforge.net/. Accessed 11 August 2013

10. http://dom4j.sourceforge.net/. Accessed 11 August 2013
11. http://traas.sf.net/. Accessed 11 August 2013
12. Schubert, T., Krumnow, M., Bäker, B., Krimmling, J.: Using nanoscopic simulations to validate the benefit of advanced driver assistance systems in complex traffic scenarios. In: 3rd International Conference on Models and Technologies for Intelligent Transportation Systems, Dresden (2013)

# SUMOPy: An Advanced Simulation Suite for SUMO

Joerg Schweizer[(✉)]

DICAM-Transportation Group, University of Bologna,
Viale Risorgimento 2, 40136 Bologna, Italy
Joerg.Schweizer@unibo.it

**Abstract.** SUMOPy is intended to (1) expand the user-base of SUMO - Simulation of Urban MObility: by providing a user-friendly, yet flexible simulation suite for SUMO, including a GUI and scripting; (2) enhance the demand modeling capacity, in particular by providing an activity-based demand modeling and making more extensive use of the attributes provided by the OpenStreetMap database; (3) easier management of existing vehicle types such as bicycles as well as new vehicle types like Personal Rapid Transit (PRT). The vision of SUMOPy is to simulate a synthetic population in a multi-modal transport environment, because it is believed that only in this way the net-effect of new transport modes and technologies can be assessed. The basic architecture and principles of operation are explained and some examples on how to use SUMOPy through both, GUI and scripting are presented. SUMOPy is still in an early stage of development and many of the current SUMO capabilities are not yet implemented. However this article explains which features will be added in the near future and how they fit in the existing structure.

**Keywords:** SUMO · Python · Micro-simulation · Synthetic population · OpenStreetMap · PRT · GRT

## 1 Introduction

SUMO - Simulation of Urban Mobility [1], rapidly developed into a flexible and powerful open-source micro-simulator for multi-modal urban traffic networks [2]. The features and the number of tools provided are constantly increasing, making simulations ever more realistic. At the present state, the different functionalities consist of a large number of binaries and scripts that act upon a large number of files, containing information on the network, the vehicles, districts, trips routes, configurations, and many other parameters. Scripts (mostly written in Python), binaries and data files exist in a dispersed manner. The flow of data processing is illustrated in Fig. 1(a).

In practice, a master script is necessary which holds all processes and data together as to simulate a specific scenario in a controlled way. This approach is extremely flexible, but it can become very time consuming and error prone to find the various tools, combine their input and output and generate the various configuration files. Furthermore, it reduces the user-base of SUMO to those familiar with scripting and command line interfaces. Instead, SUMO has the potential to become a multi-disciplinary

© Springer-Verlag Berlin Heidelberg 2014
M. Behrisch et al. (Eds.): SUMO 2013, LNCS 8594, pp. 71–82, 2014.
DOI: 10.1007/978-3-662-45079-6_6

simulation platform if it becomes more accessible to disciplines and competences outside the field of computer science.

This problem has been recognized and different graphical user interfaces have been developed. The traffic modeler (also named traffic generator) is a tool written in Java which helps to manage files, configure simulations and to evaluate and visualize results. SUMOPy is written entirely in the object-oriented script language Python, it uses wxWindows as GUI interface and NumPy for fast numerical array-type calculations. SUMOPy is similar to the traffic generator in that it simplifies the use of SUMO through a GUI. But SUMOPy is more than just a GUI, it is a suite that allows to access SUMO tools and binaries in a simple unified fashion. The distinguishing features are:

- SUMOPy has Python instances that can make direct use of most functions tools already available as Python code. This avoids time consuming writing and parsing after each step, as illustrated in Fig. 1(b). However, intermediate results are still obtained by writing and parsing files, as shown in Sect. 2.1.
- SUMOPy has a Python command line interface that allows direct and interactive manipulation of SUMOPy instances.
- SUMOPy provides a library that greatly simplifies the scripting.

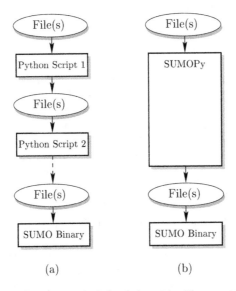

**Fig. 1.** Illustration of data flow in a typical simulation, (a) with current SUMO distribution, (b) the *idealized* flow with SUMOPy extension.

The paper is organized as follows: Sect. 2 is a brief summary of the principles of operation, where data are stored, which functions are available, including the (current) SUMOPy file tree; Sect. 3 explains the GUI and Sect. 4 gives some brief scripting examples. Section 5 draws preliminary conclusions of the current SUMOPy development.

## 2 Principles of Operation

The principles of operation of SUMOPy is that functions, processes or methods act upon a central data structure, called the *Scenario*, that holds together all necessary information to prepare and generate data to run a SUMO micro-simulation and to process its results (see Fig. 2). Dependent on the specific study, the user must provide certain input data to the scenario, other input data can be generated and completed by applying dedicated functions and methods. The scenario structure is shown below (Sect. 2.1) and the main functions are briefly explained in the following Sect. 2.2, while the directories and files of SUMOPy are explained in Sect. 2.3. Both, scenario data and functions can be accessed or executed via GUI (see Sect. 3) or scripting (see Sect. 4).

### 2.1 The Scenario Data Structure

The main data elements of the scenario are shown in Fig. 2. The parts in gray are planned and not implemented at the time of writing this article. The main instances of the scenario are: net, demand, vehicle types and results. A major future extension will be a land-use structure which allows to generate a synthetic population.

Most of the data in Fig. 2 are instances (except python primitives), that provide specific attributes and basic methods to add, get, set and delete the data they contain.

- *Network*: the network containing edges, lanes, nodes/junctions, connections, traffic-lights and roundabouts. The network instance is compatible with the network instance provided with the SUMO Toolbox, but has many enhancements. The network can be read and written into the native SUMO net file format.
- *Demand*: the demand instance holds all data and methods necessary to generate trips and routes. The central idea is that the trips, generated from different generation models (example: OD demand, turn-ratio demand, random trip generators and public transport lines) can be superimposed in a flexible manner. With the Origin-To-Destination matrices (ODMs) one can specify the number of trips between districts for specific time intervals and vehicle classes. This data can be exported to ODM files in XML format. Districts are defined in the traffic assignment zones (TAZ), which is editable through the GUI. From the ODM data one can generate trips with the ODM to trips function and then use the Duarouter to produce the routes.Turn-ratio based demand can be given by flows per edge (this is the generated flow) and the flows in each direction at junctions to specify how the generated flows split up at reach junction. The vehicles (which represent the travel modes) is a currently simply a table with vehicle types and their specific parameters. Parameters can be edited through the GUI and saved in a XML file.
- *Results*: instance contains all output data from the simulation and provides methods to read and collect them. There are currently 2 structures implemented: edge oriented data and trip-oriented data. The edge data can be displayed with the GUI and examined interactively.

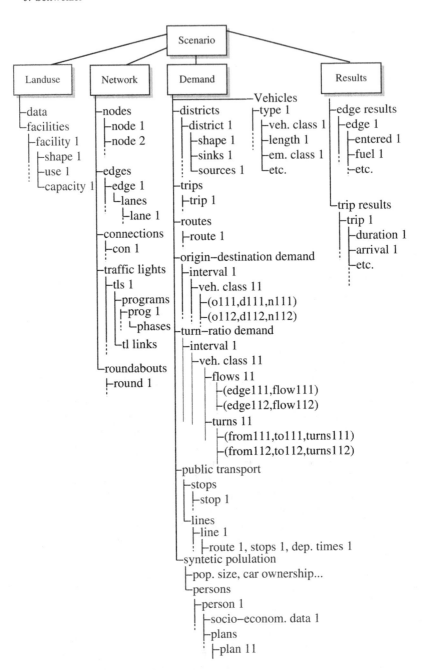

**Fig. 2.** Data structure of the scenario, the central instance in SUMOPy, truncated at irrelevant branches. Demand structure is shown in more detail. Gray parts are future extensions.

The planned data-structures (Fig. 2 in grey) are:

- A land-use data structure, holding geo-referenced facilities (buildings, areas) and their respective use plus other transport relevant attributes.
- A demand instance that allows to add public transport stops and public transport lines (also through GUI).
- A demand instance that holds a virtual population. This is an important path towards activity based trip chaining in a multi-modal network simulation. The generator will make use of the land-use data structure too.
- More result types: time dependent edge and trip data.

Note that SUMOPy manages all files involved in a scenario, including naming reading and parsing whenever necessary, see Sect. 2.2.

## 2.2   Main Functions, Methods and Processes

Functions, methods and processes provided by the SUMOPy library can change and add data to the scenario. Methods within a main instance focus on adding/deleting and retrieving data, while keeping consistency with other data under the same structure. In addition, the scenario instance provides a large number of standard methods to import/export and transform data, including the SUMO micro-simulation. Some methods are either entirely written in Python (functions provided either by the SUMOPY library or from SUMO tools); or the methods dumps data to files, runs a SUMO binary and parses from output files back into the scenario data structure.

For more complex or long-lasting operations, a process instance is created, which lives at least for the duration of the process. The process can call other functions and check their input and output. The process can be run as a separate threat or in the background (nohup still experimental). The currently implemented main scenario methods are:

- Import from osm: function to download and convert a network of any size from the OSM server (note that the quality of the OSM network may vary significantly). Input for this function is the bounding box or the area code. A network and polygon xml file will be generated. This is just a convenience function for already implemented functions in the SUMO import toolbox.
- Network generator: the standard SUMO network generator can be accessed directly through python.
- Make TAZ: generates traffic assignment zones from district and edge information. Uses modified functions from SUMO district toolbox.
- Odm to trips: function to generate trips from the data contained in the district-to-district-oriented origin-destination demand data structure, entirely written in python, using some modified functions from the SUMO district toolbox.
- Dua route: runs standard SUMO router to produce routes from trip information.
- JTR router: to produce routes from turn ratio information.
- Dua iterate: wrapper around the python script duaiterate provided by the SUMO toolbox.

Note that the above methods are scenario class methods and called from within python. The underlying writing of configuration files and updating of internal data is taken care of by the scenario instance. Function parameters to configure a particular function can be passed as input arguments for the python method.

Future extensions include:

- Import for different network file formats (make a better use of netconvert and OD2TRIPS).
- Random trip generator (already implemented in SUMO toolbox).
- TraCI Interface: runs a SUMO simulation which is controlled by SUMOPy through the Traffic Control Interface (TraCI). There are already python scripts available that will be integrated into the SUMOPy framework. Also easy to use custom control modules will be included.
- Rapid Transit (PRT) and Group Rapid Transit (GRT) control: one control module via TraCI will allow special PRT and GRT vehicle types to receive demand dependent routing. Such vehicles would stop at the stations and pick up or unload persons. If not used, they are automatically routed to another stop with demand or to a depot.

### 2.3   Directories and Files

The SUMOPy directory contains currently the main python file to run SUMOPy in graphical interface mode (sumopy_gui.py) and the main sumopy classes and methods (sumopy.py), including the scenario, duaroute, jtrrouter, etc. The other directories have the following contents:

- lib_meta contains universal class management and import/export methods that are *not* SUMO specific. The main library is called classmanager, which provides a set of Mixin classes that allow the management of a class and it attributes, including reading/ saving, standard exports, labeling, naming and handling (deleting, inserting) of numpy array structures. Another important class is the process class which is a general framework to control a complex sequence of function calls, including file management.
- lib_meta_wx contains generic, *not* SUMO specific, GUI classes such as an object browser and a canvas editor, using the wxPython library (A python wrapper for wxWindows). These are mainly widgets to represent objects that inherit the class manager methods in the lib_meta.
- lib_sumopy is the directory which contains modules with all SUMOPy compatible functions and processes. Some files are copies of modules found in the SUMO/tools directory, but with different function-call procedures. The sub-directories and files in more detail:
  - lib_demand: contains all demand related methods.
    - Odm: contains all origin-to-destination related demand methods.
      - Odm.py: structure and methods to manipulate ODM data plus reading and writing data in XML.
      - Genodm.py: method to generate trips from ODM data
    - Turnflows: contains turn ratio-related demand methods

- Turnflows.py: structure and methods to manipulate Turn ratio data plus reading and writing data in XML.
- Demand.py: is the main demand instance holding all other demand components together.
- Vehicles.py: Vehicles structure and methods.
- Zones.py: Contains all district-related structures and methods, including the function to determine the set of edges in each defined district (edgeIn Districts).
- Lib_network: network related structures and functions.
  - Network.py: Contains Network class, including edges, lanes, nodes, connections, etc.
  - Netgenerate.py: functions to generate artificial SUMO networks.
- Lib_processes: collection of more complex processes that act upon data structures of both, network and demand (and that are not implemented in sumopy.py itself).
  - dualterate.py: iterative SUMO/duaroute function (a modified function of the module with the same name in the SUMO/tools directory)
  - osm.py: main process class and methods to download and convert osm data.
  - osmBuild.py/osmGet: same functions as module in SUMO/tools directory. There have been small modifications and extensions regarding function calls and file naming.
  - Sumo.py: process class of sumo simulation.
- resultslib.py: contains results classes and methods to read, write and represent edge and trip-oriented result data.
- lib_sumopy_wx: SUMOPy specific GUI classes built on the classes provided in lib_meta_wx.
  - netview2.py: Currently the only module, which contains network and results viewing widget. Actually each visible network or demand object in the network. py library has a "sister object" in this library, which represents its graphical appearance. These graphical sister objects are updated through event call-backs if attributes of the network object changes.

# 3  Graphical User Interface

The main window consist of three main elements: an *object browser*; *the network/ results viewer* and a *command line interface (CLI)*, as shown in Fig. 3.

The object browser is a powerful tool that allows to browse through all instances and child instances of a scenario. It is further possible to change some parameters interactively. All tables can be exported in CSV format.

The network viewer is interactive and single edges and nodes can be examined in combination with the object browser. Some edge and lane attributes, like maximum speed or access restrictions can be changed. Zooming further into the network shown also the lanes and connections between them (see Fig. 4). There the network viewer provides also limited network editing capabilities like deletion, moving and modifying links, lanes, lanes nodes and connections. Also districts can be manually created and modified.

The command line interface allows to interact with the scenario objects through Python commands. The interface includes a help for typing by prompting with a list of class methods and options to choose from.

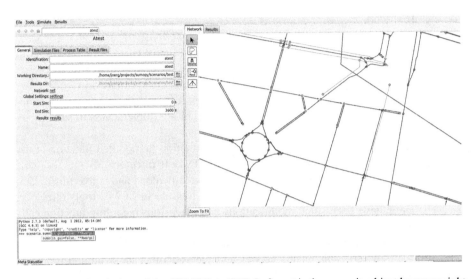

**Fig. 3.** The main window of the SUMOPy's GUI: Left part is the scenario object browser; right part the network/results viewer where roads are in blue, bicycle lanes in green, delivery access roads in dark blue, nodes (junctions) in cyan; below in interactive command line interface.

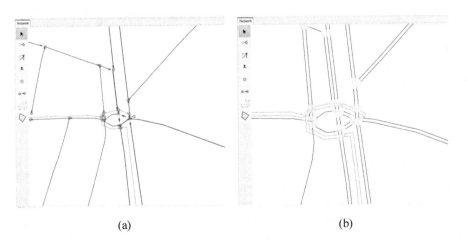

(a)                                                      (b)

**Fig. 4.** Viewing and editing capabilities: (a) Nodes/edges zoom level. (b) Connections/lanes zoom level.

The main functions, like trip-generation and routing are menu driven. More complex functions like Open Street Map import, ODM editing or the SUMO simulation are processes and do have their own GUI as shown in (see Figs. 5 and 6).

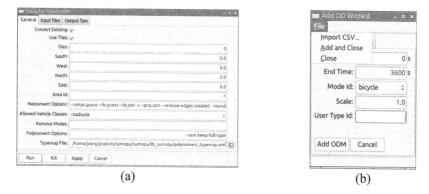

(a)                                           (b)

**Fig. 5.** (a) Dialog to download and import OSM data (using netconvert), including conversion of buildings (using polyconvert). (b) Dialog to import origin to destination data in csv format for a specific mode and time period.

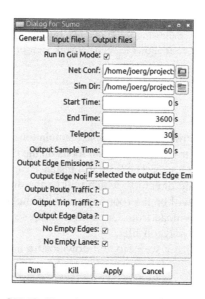

**Fig. 6.** Dialog to run SUMO. Note the options to generate different kinds of output.

The result fewer maps edge and trip oriented simulation results onto the network, see Fig. 7. Edge oriented results can be examined interactively together with the object viewer.

The quality of the result view will be improved by adding scales and options how results are displayed.

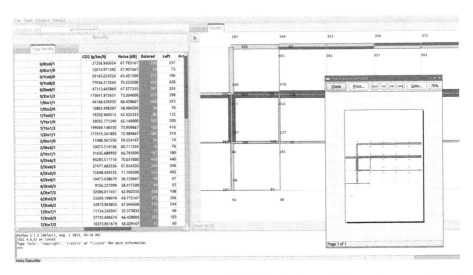

**Fig. 7.** Left side: object browser showing result in table. Background: interactive network result viewer. Foreground: print previewer allows to send network view or results view to printer or pdf file.

## 4  Scripting

Scripting with SUMOPy allows to write complex simulation macros with a few lines of code with the effect that the traffic engineer can focus on the planning/modeling process rather than on programming issues. The Scenario instance can be initialized by giving a scenario name and a working directory, which will be the directory where all files are stored. The scenario name will be the root name of all simulation files. The following lines initiate a scenario, download from Open Street Map server (OSM) and convert it into a SUMO network and polygon file:.

Example code to initialize a scenario and download a network from Open street:

```
scenario=SumoScenario('my_scenario', 'my_scenario_dir')
scenario.import_osm(bbox=[44.451,11.2864,44.533,11.4007])
```

Districts, demand and vehicle types can be added successively to the scenario by calling the respective methods. Trip- and route generations are both methods of the scenario. The command to run SUMO while producing files for various outputs (equivalent to the dialog shown in Fig. 6), is shown below.

Example code for running a SUMO simulation, simulating for one hour and generating different types of output:

```
scenario.sumo( simtime_start = 0, simtime_end = 3600,
          is_tripinfo = True,      # Trips output
          is_edgedata = False,     # no Edges output
          is_lanedata = False,      # no Lane output
          is_edgeemissions = True,  # Edge emissions
          is_edgenoise = False,     # no Edge noise
          )
```

The results (here trip data and edge noise) will be read from the output files into the result data structure (see Fig. 2) from where it can be viewed. In particular all data is stored in NumPy arrays which allows a fast post processing.

Current work in progress is to make changes to the network through the command line interface immediately visible in the network viewer and result viewer through appropriate callback functions.

## 5 Conclusions

The basic concepts and architecture of SUMOPy have been outlined and the GUI as well as the scripting possibilities have been explained. Evidently the current version does only support a subset of SUMO's potentials. Nevertheless, we have shown the next steps how SUMOPy can be extended to a user-friendly, yet flexible multimodal traffic micro-simulator. In any case, the basic SUMO file formats will be maintained, which means that a scenario produced by SUMOPy can also by simulated without the use of SUMOPy.

The main development priorities are the TraCI module (with PRT and GRT vehicle controls). Also the implementation of a virtual population would be an important step towards more realistic user models.

Yet, even with all the proposed extensions, SUMOPy is unlikely to compete with commercial micro-simulators. But its strength will be its openness and transparent architecture, which invites to implement specialized transport systems (like ITS, PRT or GRT) and test them within a complex transport demand scenarios.

SUMOPy has the potential to make SUMO accessible to a wider user group as it allows transport planners to work more on the transport problem and sophisticated demand models rather than on programming issues. On the other hand, ITS specialists may have the opportunity to draw on more realistic scenarios. This means SUMOPy may become an important interdisciplinary bridge which may diffuse traffic micro-simulations and its connected transport technologies to a larger scientific community.

## References

1. Behrisch, M., Bieker, L., Erdmann, J., Krajzewicz, D.: SUMO - simulation of Urban MObility: an overview. In: SIMUL 2011, The Third International Conference on Advances in System Simulation (2011)

2. Krajzewicz, D., Hartinger, M., Hertkorn, G., Mieth, P., Rössel, C., Wagner, P., Ringel, J.: The "Simulation of Urban MObility" package: an open source traffic simulation. In: 2003 European Simulation and Modeling Conference (2003)
3. Traffic modeler home page. http://trafficmodeler.sourceforge.net/

# 3D Visualization for Microscopic Traffic Data Sources

Matthew Fullerton[1(✉)], Andreas Wenger[2], Mathias Baur[1],
Florian Schimandl[1], Jonas Lüßmann[1], and Silja Hoffmann[1]

[1] Chair of Traffic Engineering and Control,
Technische Universität München, Munich, Germany
`{matthew.fullerton,mathias.baur,florian.schimandl,`
`jonas.luessmann,silja.hoffmann}@tum.de`
[2] Xenoage Software, Schrobenhausen, Germany
`andi@xenoage.com`

**Abstract.** The typical approach to realistic 3D visualization of microscopic traffic data is usually location-specific and hence requires a lot of effort from the user to generate an eye-pleasing model. We present a simulation/location/data-neutral 3D visualization software module that allows the 3D display of an XML-coded road network, vehicles and communication involving vehicles. These objects are automatically modeled from source data with empty space filled in an intelligent way. The simulation can be freely explored in time and space. Vehicles can be color-coded, viewed from above or from the driver's perspective, or alternatively in a traditional 2D form. Furthermore, online statistics on the current vehicle's and traffic state of the can be configured and displayed.

**Keywords:** Microscopic traffic simulation · Data visualization · 3D visualization

## 1 Introduction

### 1.1 Motivation

Microscopic traffic simulation has become an established tool for the examination of microscopic level "what if" questions in traffic engineering [1]. These can include proposed infrastructure changes, changes in traffic regulation, and devices in traffic providing communication between vehicles for purposes of improved traffic safety or efficiency. Although the critical outcomes of simulation are usually 'hard' numbers (such as average speeds, travel times, traffic flows), visualization of some kind is essential for purposes of visual validation and debugging. In both science and industry, 3D visualizations have become more popular: driver and traffic behavior is easier to judge, the viewer is more engaged in the presentation and the display invites exploration and questions. Hence such visualizations are useful both for demonstration and teaching.

### 1.2 Background

For a traffic simulation, we usually only configure roads, junctions, traffic lights etc. There may also be objects in the simulation that correspond to real world objects, but

© Springer-Verlag Berlin Heidelberg 2014
M. Behrisch et al. (Eds.): SUMO 2013, LNCS 8594, pp. 83–96, 2014.
DOI: 10.1007/978-3-662-45079-6_7

they are somewhat abstracted (for example, a network link with reduced speed might actually correspond to an overhead motorway control sign). Overall, the normal simulation objects are not enough to generate a realistic and attractive 3D visualization, where viewers probably expect other real-world items such as safety barriers, vegetation and buildings. In addition, with the trend towards simulating communication amongst vehicles and infrastructure [2], we have data on communication that we also want to see in a simulation visualization. As tools for simulating communication are usually in the form of add-on modules that interface with the simulation tool (e.g. VSimRTI [3], iTETRIS [2]), the communication is not usually displayed in the simulation user interface. This abstraction also motivates the choice for the visualization to also be abstracted and separated from the simulation tool: modern questions of traffic engineering, in particular vehicular communication, may require a greater diversity of simulation tools, if only for verification in what is still a relatively young field [4]. We know of no popular microscopic traffic simulator that visualizes the communication between vehicles as part of the normal visualization. SUMO [5] in particular lacks any kind of 3D visualization, either online during the simulation or offline based on the simulation log file.

Furthermore, in modern traffic engineering, we also have access to other data with a similar level of detail as microscopic simulation results, such as Floating Car Data (FCD) or trajectories from video analysis. Given visualization software that only requires a network description and the trajectories of vehicles, there is no reason why these data can also not be viewed in the same animated, 3D format.

## 1.3   Solution

To resolve these issues, we have developed a software tool, vtSim.VIEW that visualizes any road network, set of vehicle trajectories upon it and communication between entities. The data source for the visualization is a simple XML; to assist in generating this from simulation tool data, the vtSim data and simulation management framework [4] can be used, but it acts only as a bridge and is not required to use the software. Based on the road network, the module automatically generates much of the road environment and surroundings that are not defined in the simulation network: no 3D modeling is required on the part of the user, although structures can be added for decoration (see Sect. 4.2). Although the visualization is offline in the sense that the simulation is performed independent of the visualization (only the data describing the network and vehicle trajectories are required), it is performed in real time based on this data, hence not requiring any advance video rendering before viewing. It should be stressed that the visualization is in no way a traffic simulator and is fully independent of whatever vehicle or communication models were used in the simulation. This also has the advantage that for slower-than-real-time simulations (as is often the case when communication between vehicles is included), the visualization is not delayed and can be viewed and reviewed from any viewpoint at the preferred speed.

## 1.4    Outline

The paper is structured as follows: first an overview of the software's features is given. This is followed by a description of the data format, an overview of the tool's usage, and details of the implementation, including how the source data are interpreted and displayed. We conclude with an outlook towards future work.

# 2    Features

In summary, vtSim.VIEW offers the following features:

- Reading simulation networks for rural (highway, Figs. 1, 2, 3) and urban scenarios (Fig. 6)
- Editing roads and surroundings like trees, houses or traffic infrastructure by means of a dedicated editor (Fig. 11)
- Animating vehicles, roads and their environment using detailed 3D models
- Different freely definable camera viewpoints (including birds-eye view and ego-perspective)
- Showing application-specific attributes like message transmission visualization or warning display
- Online plotting of traffic related parameters during visualization run.

**Fig. 1.** Display of communication attributes in the visualization for the case of a traffic jam warning

**Fig. 2.** Display of application attributes in the visualization for the case of a traffic jam warning

One of the features of vtSim.VIEW is the visualization of message transmission between objects (see Fig. 1) and the illustration of the entities (usually vehicles) internal state (message received, information shown to the driver etc.; see Fig. 2). Additionally, different elements of static road side equipment (side rails, gantries containing direction signs, sign posts etc.) as well as dynamic road side equipment (gantries with variable message signs, traffic signals and signal states for vehicles and pedestrians) can be displayed easily within the scenarios.

The driver-perspective camera view offers the viewer the possibility to stay in one vehicle while displaying the essential information on a freely configurable dashboard (see Fig. 3).

## 3 Data Model

### 3.1 Workflow

The primary data necessary for vtSim.VIEW are first a set of XML SUMO-format network source files (node, edge and connection descriptions) and second a description (also in XML) of the vehicle data. These need to be created by the user (e.g. through conversion scripts) based on the simulation output (trajectories and communication) or other data source. Currently, tools are available to convert data from VISSIM (extensive) and SUMO (vehicle movements only). A typical workflow is summarized

**Fig. 3.** Driver view while approaching a work zone.

in Fig. 4. It shows the workflow of the visualization. The network used for simulation along with the simulation vehicle trajectories log and communications log from the simulated application are prepared as XML files for the vtSim.VIEW visualization tool. This can either be done by the user as part of their results-handling process or achieved using vtSim.

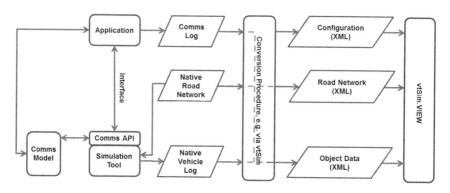

**Fig. 4.** Visualization workflow

### 3.2 Files Used

In order to run a simulated scene in the visualisation environment, there needs to be a basic configuration of the scenes, the underlying network and data sources for the simulated vehicles and dynamic infrastructure components. For that purpose, vtSim.

VIEW uses a folder structure inside of a "data" folder where (almost, see below) all user files should be deposited. Table 1 shows a list of all used data file formats in vtSim.VIEW.

**Table 1.** Files for vtSim.VIEW

| Format | Directory | Extensions | Meaning |
|---|---|---|---|
| Scene | data/scene/ | .scene.xml | When opening vtSim.VIEW, the user selects a scene. A scene consists of a Map, Simulation data, cameras and some additional meta information |
| Map | data/map/ | .map.xml | A map contains the static geometry of a scene. This includes the street net, terrain and other objects. A map can be edited using the Editor mode of vtSim.VIEW |
| SUMO street net | data/net/ | .con.xml<br>.edg.xml<br>.nod.xml | The street information in SUMO format. vtSim.VIEW expects little modifications in the format, which are described in this chapter |
| Simulation | data/simulation/ | .simulation.xml | A simulation contains information on vehicles, traffic lights and other objects over time. It has a start and end time. A construction site and custom cockpit dashboard can be defined |
| Vehicle tracking | data/tracking/ | .tracking.xml | Tracking data (position over time, meta information,…) of vehicles |
| VISSIM traffic lights program | data/trafficlights/ | .lsa | VISSIM.lsa file for traffic light programs. We will work to make this file less simulator-specific in the future (see below) |
| Cockpit dashboard | data/dashboard/ | .dashboard.xml | Layout of the generic dashboard in the driver's cockpit. There may be instruments like a speed indicator, a warning display, logo images and so on |

The road network is coded in XML, broadly in accordance with the SUMO XML specification [6]. This specification is well documented and acts as a standard for the current vtSim software. Three XML files are required;.nod.xml representing road network nodes,.edg.xml representing road network edges (links) and.con.xml describing the connections between links. As we use both VISSIM [7] and SUMO [5] in our work, some parameters were added for preserving the geometry of edge connections (or in VISSIM terminology, connectors between links), which, unlike in SUMO, can have non-negligible lengths, geometries and must not necessarily begin or end at the start- or end-point of an edge. However, the data format used was intended to provide for SUMO compatibility.

The addition of communication and driver warning displays (system-specific) is achieved with additional XML-elements like "sending" for indicating a vehicle currently sending out a message via vehicular communication capabilities, "receiving" for a vehicle receiving such a message and "status" for indicating a vehicles warning (Table 2).

**Table 2.** Possible message contents

| System (type) | Message content (content) | Possible statuses |
|---|---|---|
| Congestion warning ("Congestion") | Distance in meters | "warned", "in_jam", "cam_jam_recognition" |
| Construction warning ("Construction") | Distance in meters | "warned" |
| Obstacle warning ("BDV" for "broken down vehicle" – may be renamed later to reflect its more general purpose) | Distance in meters, type of obstacle | "warned" |
| Green light advisory – remaining time to red light ("restred") | Remaining red time in seconds | None (tag not used) |
| Green light optimized speed advisory ("speedadvice") | Advised speed in km/h | None (tag not used) |

According to the warning/system type, a different HMI can be shown.

In addition to system-specific dashboard information, other information can be provided for either dash-board display or plotting. Several other xml files state which files are required and which camera positions will be available.

In the simplest case, a final tracking data file including communications and vehicle data can be output directly in the correct format. However, usually vehicle and communication simulation are well separated and and need to be converted and combined. In our work, we output an internally-standardized intermediary format for communications data from simulated applications (these are connected to the simulation but the simulation has no knowledge of their internal function and hence does not output any data concerning them). This is then "merged" with the trajectory data output from the simulation to create the tracking file using a Python script.

Handling Traffic Lights and Cockpit view data. vtSim.VIEW is able handle dynamic traffic light information concerning signal phase changing times. At the moment, the necessary data format is the VISSIM signal phase and timing output (VISSIM output files with the suffix.lsa). Although conversion from other simulation tools is possible (the VISSIM traffic light output is basically a simple csv file), we hope to move to a more generic format in the future.

As the view can be dynamically switched from the bird's eye view perspective to the vehicle's cockpit view, vtSim.VIEW offers displays options for the dashboard and the warning/information display (human-machine–interface). This dashboard can be configured by editing a dedicated dashboard XML file. This can include up to 3 rows of text; currently, values detailing the current acceleration value and the current time gap in seconds to the leading vehicle are available (these are taken from the tracking file, not calculated by the software). A styled speed indicator in km/h can be shown (see Fig. 3), as well as an image indicating if a warning is present (see Fig. 3), and another image (i.e. system branding).

## 4  Usage

When starting vtSim.VIEW, a window pictured in Fig. 5 appears.

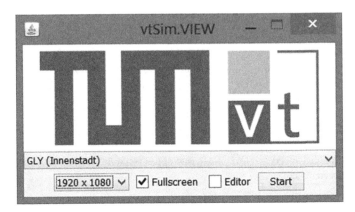

**Fig. 5.** The initial window allows selection of scenario, screen resolution and mode (editor or not)

The user can select a scene and some display options (screen resolution and full-screen mode). Furthermore, vtSim.VIEW can be started in Visualization mode or in Editor mode (when the "Editor" checkbox is selected).

### 4.1  Visualization Mode

Figure 6 shows a screenshot of the visualization, showing an urban scene. All available windows and controls are shown. Normally, only the bottom bar is visible.

The bottom bar contains various controls:

- A click on the "Help [F1]" button or the "F1" shortcut key shows an overview over the available shortcuts (see also Fig. 7).
- The current "Time" can be freely selected using the slider on the left.
- "Speed" can be altered using the speed slider. 100 % means, that 1 real second is 1 simulation second, 200 % means, that 1 real second is 2 simulation seconds.
- The simulation can be paused at any time using the "Pause" button.
- The pre-defined cameras can be activated by selecting an element from the cameras dropdown. Where shortcuts are defined, those are shown in brackets (like "Bird's Eye [1]", when "1" is the shortcut key for this camera).
- A click on the "Options" button shows the display options (see also Fig. 8). These are described later.

Currently, navigation is accomplished with keyboard control. The possible actions are listed in Fig. 7. The "up" and "down" arrow keys have different meanings dependent on the view. Normally, they rotate the view to the top or to the bottom. In the Map view (2D view), they zoom in and out.

**Fig. 6.** Visualization mode

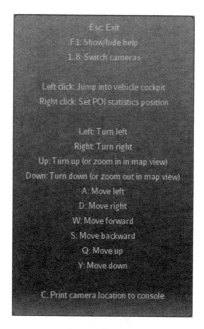

**Fig. 7.** Help

The Options window (Fig. 8) gives the user more control over the display:

- "Show legend" shows the legend for the color-coded mode.
- "Show cockpit statistics" shows a statistics window (see Fig. 6, at the top-left corner). It is filled with data when the Cockpit view is active.

- "Show POI statistics" shows another statistics window (see Fig. 6, under the cockpit statistics window). It is filled with data when a "POI statistics position" has been placed, which captures data of the vehicles driving through it. It can be placed with a right mouse click (see Fig. 7).
- "Color-coded map" switches the display of the map from realistic mode to color-coded mode. For example, color-coded mode may be better in 2D view.
- "Color-coded vehicles" switches between realistic vehicle coloring and and color-coded mode. For example, Fig. 6 shows vehicles in color-coded mode. The colors provide information about the state of the vehicles (Fig. 9).
- "Stretch map view" applies only in the Map view (2D view). The projection is stretched on the x-axis, so that a larger area can be displayed, without making the streets thinner on the y-axis. For example, this can be useful to observe the vehicles on a long, straight street.

**Fig. 8.** Options

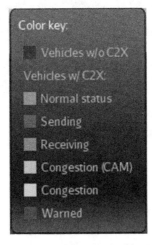

**Fig. 9.** Legend for color-coded vehicles

**Fig. 10.** Editing a road element to create a bridge within a rural scenario.

## 4.2 Editor Mode

When starting a scene in the Editor mode (Fig. 10) additional predefined objects like trees, buildings or street markings can be added to (or removed from) the map, To move, rotate or scale the objects, buttons can be used.

There are three rows of controls, two at the top and one at the bottom.

- First row at the top:
  - "Save map as…" asks the user for a map file name and saves the current state
  - "Editor mode" switches between "Edit objects" mode (described here) and the "Edit Streets" mode (described in the next paragraph)

- Second row at the top:
  - The left dropdown and button add objects to the map, like trees and buildings
  - The right dropdown and button add markings, like crosswalks or arrows

- Bottom row:
  - "Clone": The selected object is cloned
  - "Remove": The selected object is deleted
  - "Move", dropdown, "Backw", "Forw", "Left", "Right": Moves the selected object by the distance selected in the dropdown
  - "Rotate", dropdown, "Left", "Right": Rotates the selected object by the angle selected in the dropdown
  - "Scale", dropdown, "+", "-": Scales the selected object by the zooming factor in the dropdown.

It is also possible to edit road elements, which is useful for rural maps, when bridges should be created. For the visualization the road elements can be given a label (ground, ramp or bridge) and the height of the starting and ending point can be edited. Using the "Update" buttons marking lines, verges, crash barriers and bridges are visualized according to the street levels.

## 5  Implementation

### 5.1  Language Choice and Libraries Used

The software is written in Java, ensuring runtime compatibility with all desktop platforms. The fact that most popular traffic simulations are not written in Java is not a problem because of the modular structure of vtSim and vtSim.VIEW where data-transfer is achieved via files. SUMO in particular already takes an extensible approach to simulation whereby the core software is written in C++ but some additional tools provided are written in Java or Python, and an online control interface for external applications is provided [5]. For 3D rendering, the open-source jMonkeyEngine [8] is used, which comes with some free models including the car object used. It also allows the display of all kinds of 3D models compatible with the free modeling software Blender [9], such as other objects that were acquired from the commercial model library TurboSquid [10]. The complete program architecture is shown in Fig. 11.

### 5.2  Visualization

The conversion from the network representation to a 3D graphic is performed by first building a wireframe model based on the network description. Connections to other

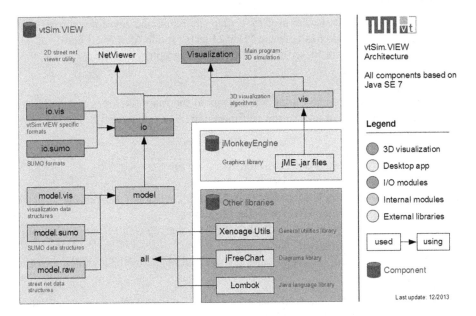

**Fig. 11.** vtSim.VIEW software architecture

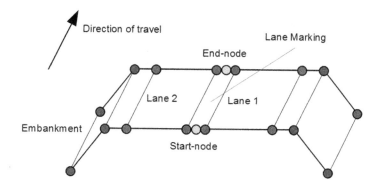

**Fig. 12.** Schematic diagram of road link construction.

links and the number of lanes are taken into account. Figure 12 shows the construction of a road section schematically.

The edges of roads are augmented appropriately for the scenario. For the rural scenario, empty land is shown as grass featuring undulating hills and the sky is textured. Vehicles are shown with detailed vehicle models. The size of the network displayed by vtSim.VIEW is only limited by system memory. Efficient culling techniques in the jMonkeyEngine compute only the geometry which is actually visible on the screen.

## 6  Outlook

The creation of a tool for generic, realistic 3D visualization based only the simulation geometry, vehicle trajectories and (optionally) vehicular communication data has rapidly accelerated the process of creating life-like 3D material for exploration and display. The software is aimed at those in research and industry who require realistic visualizations that do not need to exactly reflect the exact geography of the modelled location. Likewise, the software can add realism to generic simulations (e.g. vehicular communication system prototyping) that are not based on any real road network.

We have already used the software to great effect in the research projects simTD [11], SOCIONICAL [12] and ecoMove [13], using source data from the VISSIM [7] simulator and data derived from video recordings. By using a well-described, XML-based data format, the software is not specific to any one data source, simulated or otherwise.

We intend to extend the software to handle pedestrians, cyclists and road-side communication units. We may consider using information beyond edges and their shapes (which are normally enough for a motorway network) such as the shapes of junctions in the simulation, where available.

# References

1. Barceló, J.: Fundamentals of Traffic Simulation. Springer, Heidelberg (2010)
2. Härri, J., Cataldi, P., Krajzewicz, D., Blokpoel, R. J., Lopez, Y., Leguay, J., Bieker, L.: Modeling and simulating ITS applications with iTETRIS. In: Proceedings of the 6th ACM workshop on Performance monitoring and measurement of heterogeneous wireless and wired networks, pp. 33–40. ACM, New York (2011)
3. Rieck, D., Schünemann, B., Radusch, I., Meinel, C.: Efficient traffic simulator coupling in a distributed V2X simulation environment. In: Proceedings of the 3rd International ICST Conference on Simulation Tools and Techniques, Article No. 72. ICST, Brussels (2010)
4. Baur, M., Fullerton, M., Busch, F.: Realizing an effective and flexible ITS evaluation strategy through modular and multi-scaled traffic simulation. Intell. Transp. Syst. Mag. **2**, 34–42 (2010)
5. Krajzewicz, D.: Traffic simulation with SUMO - Simulation of Urban Mobility. In: Barceló, J. (ed.) Fundamentals of Traffic Simulation. International Series in Operations Research and Management Science, pp. 269–294. Springer, Heidelberg (2010)
6. SUMO User Documentation - Networks/Building Networks from own XML-descriptions. http://sumo.sourceforge.net/doc/current/docs/userdoc/Networks/Building_Networks_from_own_XML-descriptions.html
7. Fellendorf, M., Vortisch, P.: Microscopic traffic flow simulator VISSIM. In: Barceló, J. (ed.) Fundamentals of Traffic Simulation. International Series in Operations Research and Management Science, pp. 63–93. Springer, Heidelberg (2010)
8. jMonkeyEngine. http://www.jmonkeyengine.com
9. Blender. http://www.blender.org
10. TurboSquid. http://www.turbosquid.com
11. simTD, - Safe and Intelligent Mobility Test Field Germany. http://www.simtd.de/index.dhtml//-/enEN
12. SOCIONICAL - Complex socio-technical system in ambient intelligence. http://cordis.europa.eu/projects/rcn/89519_en.html
13. ECOMOVE - Cooperative Mobility Systems and Services for Energy Efficiency. http://cordis.europa.eu/projects/rcn/94140_en.html

# Applications and Surveys

# Driver Attitude and Its Influence on the Energy Waste of Electric Buses

Deborah Perrotta[1,2(✉)], José Luiz Macedo[1], Rosaldo J.F. Rossetti[1],
João Luiz Afonso[2], Zafeiris Kokkinogenis[1], and Bernardo Ribeiro[3]

[1] Laboratório de Inteligência Artificial e Ciência de Computadores,
Departamento de Engenharia Informática, Faculdade de Engenharia
da Universidade do Porto, Porto, Portugal
deborahperrotta@gmail.com,
{ei07130, rossetti, pro08017}@fe.up.pt
[2] Centro Algoritmi, Universidade do Minho, Braga, Portugal
jla@dei.uminho.pt
[3] CEIIA - Centro para a Excelência e Inovação na Indústria Automóvel,
Coimbra, Portugal
bernardo.ribeiro@ceiia.com

**Abstract.** The objective of this paper is to analyze the influence of different driver behaviors on the energy consumption of electric buses. It shows that risk-taking attitudes on traffic are not only dangerous to the driver, to the bus users and to the surroundings, but also promotes a poorer performance of the vehicle itself, increasing its energy consumption and reducing the amount of energy that can be recovered on regenerative braking.

**Keywords:** Driver attitude · Electric bus energy consumption · Electric bus performance · Risk-taking behavior

## 1 Introduction

Electric vehicles are seen as one of the key players to address the issue of global warming through its operation with zero tailpipe emissions and energy efficiency improvement. In the contemporary world, many countries are working on alternatives to replace internal combustion engine vehicles. For instance, in Europe, decision N° 406/2009/EC of the European Parliament and of the Council of 23 April 2009 asks for the effort of the Member States on the reduction of greenhouse gases emissions by 20 % until 2020 (European Union 2010).

The 2007 Intergovernmental Panel on Climate Change report concluded that greenhouse gas emissions must be reduced by 50 %–85 % by 2050 as an attempt to avoid many of the worst impacts of climate change. Reducing greenhouse gas emissions from transportation will likely require a broad range of strategies, such as increasing vehicle efficiency and reducing vehicle kilometers of travel. Public transportation can be one part of the solution (Federal Transit Administration (FTA) 2010), more specifically electric buses, which are quieter than regular buses, therefore promoting a better experience to public transport users, and also does not require much investment on infrastructure, as subways and trolleys for instance.

© Springer-Verlag Berlin Heidelberg 2014
M. Behrisch et al. (Eds.): SUMO 2013, LNCS 8594, pp. 99–108, 2014.
DOI: 10.1007/978-3-662-45079-6_8

Nowadays, there are some electric buses in operation in some parts of the world and one of the main concerns is their high weight, which is mainly due to the amount of batteries they carry in order to have an adequate operation range. Nevertheless, it is crucial to investigate ways of optimizing an electric bus operation on the urban environment, promoting an efficient performance. This could lead in the future to a reduction of the bus weight, once it would require less energy to travel the same amount of kilometers, and thus less batteries would be necessary.

When talking about the operation efficiency of internal combustion vehicles, there is one factor that plays an important role on the fuel consumption: driver behavior. However, at this point it is relevant to define what characterizes an aggressive driving style. It is known that there are three aspects of driving behavior that have been labeled as aggressive in the driving literature: (a) intentional acts of physical, verbal, or gestured aggression; (b) negative emotions (e.g. anger) while driving; and (c) risk taking (Dula and Ballard 2003). For this paper, the focus will be on the third category, namely risk taking.

The risk-taking category includes behaviors such as speeding, running red lights, weaving through traffic, maneuvering without signaling, and frequent lane changing; it also comprises the dangers from lapses of attention while driving, typical for those who use the cell phone, eat, drink, smoke, or adjust a car stereo. Any of these behaviors may occur without the presence of negative emotion or intent to harm (Dula and Geller 2003).

Generally, this type of behavior has implications on fuel consumption (for internal combustion vehicles) or energy consumption (for electric vehicles), once it is characterized for the opposite behavior of the so-called eco(logical)-driving. An ecological strategy is to anticipate what is happening ahead, and drive in such a way so as to minimize acceleration and braking, cruising at the optimal speed, and to maximize coasting time at stops (Kamal et al. 2009). In other words, it may be represented by a soft driving, especially restricting acceleration rates (Miyatake 2011).

In this paper, it is intended to analyze the implications of risk taking attitudes of a driver towards the energy consumption of electric buses when compared to regular drivers. In order to do that, a mathematical model for an electric bus powertrain was developed and further implemented on the simulation suit Simulink (a simulation package of the Matlab environment). This model was further integrated to the traffic simulator SUMO through a high-level architecture approach, allowing the bus simulated on Simulink to perform a route designed on SUMO that later gives feedback to Simulink in order to perform appropriate evaluative calculations.

## 2    Simulink Model Overview

The Electric Bus Powertrain Subsystem (EBPS) is a mathematical model of an electric bus engine implemented in MATLAB Simulink (Perrotta et al. 2012). Several modules that are used to compute specific parameters constitute the model. One of these subsystems represents the vehicle powertrain, taking into account the forces that work against its movement and the gear ratios involved. An output of this subsystem computes the amount of required energy for a driving cycle to be completed. A second subsystem is implemented that calculates the amount of energy that may be possibly recovered from the regenerative braking, taking into account the kinetic energy of the vehicle. Two other subsystems are related to the batteries and the super-capacitors, evaluating whether they are capable of absorbing the energy from the braking or not. Figure 1 illustrates the main subsystem of the model.

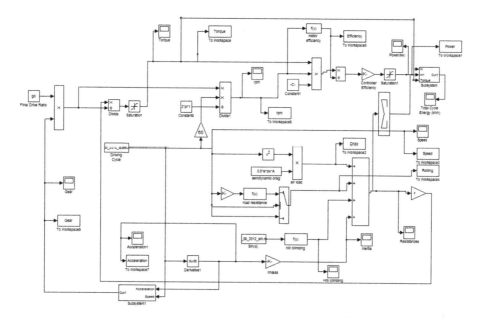

**Fig. 1.** Electric bus simulation model on Simulink

This system is modeled in continuous time. It receives a vectorial structure as input, where velocities are related to time instants. As outputs, the model produces a structure for each metric, with values associated with an instance of time. The most significant parameters calculated by this model are:

- Power: Expresses the power required for each instant of the driving cycle.
- Total Energy Cycle: Represents the energy required to complete a whole cycle.
- Braking resistance energy: It is known that electric motors are able to work in generator mode and recover part of the braking energy back to the system. This model calculates the amount of energy dissipated in braking episodes that is not available to be recovered.

## 3   Sumo

SUMO (Krajzewicz et al. 2012) is a suite of applications that are used to design and implement realistic traffic domain simulations. SUMO represents both the road network infrastructure and the traffic demand. It has become an important and popular tool within the urban traffic and transportation community.

SUMO follows the microscopic modeling approach. Thus the level of resolution is modeled with a detailed representation of the traffic dynamics. This approach will describe the behavior of the entities that make up the traffic stream as well as their interactions. In microscopic models, the level of detail scales down the individual behavior of vehicles, their interaction with each other and with the road network up to the single junction level.

To define the entity "vehicle", the modeler needs to associate it with an identifier (name), a departure time and assign it a route through the network. If it is necessary a vehicle can be further described with more details. A simulated vehicle can be associated with a type that describes the physical properties of the vehicle and the variables of the kinematic model. A pollutant or noise emission model can also be associated with each vehicle rendering the simulation more realistically. The origin/destination pairs, such as the lane to use, the speed, or the position can be defined as well. By distinguishing different vehicle types, SUMO allows the simulation of public transport or emergency vehicle prioritization at intersections.

SUMO supports the extensibility to its core and control through TraCI (Traffic Control Interface), which is an API that allows the traffic simulation to interact with an external application via a socket connection in runtime. This approach allows the application to retrieve values of simulated objects and to manipulate their behavior. TraCI has an extensive documentation of the methods for communication with SUMO. It is composed of three main sets of functions that are related to the information access, to the control of the state of objects during the simulation (e.g. speed at each step) and to the subscription of determined structure variables.

## 4   Method and Tools

An integrated simulation platform was developed in order to access the possible energy saving of regular drivers in comparison to risk-taking ones. This platform is characterized by the integration of two different simulators: a nanoscopic simulator represented by Simulink (Matlab environment), which accounts for the representation of the powertrain behavior, and a microscopic simulator represented by SUMO, which accounts for the routes that the bus is supposed to perform, the interactions of this bus with other vehicles, and the stops at bus stops and traffic lights.

### 4.1   HLA Concepts

The High Level Architecture addresses the reuse and interoperation of legacy model simulations. The HLA concept is based on the idea of the distributed simulation approach that no single simulation model can satisfy the requirements of all usages and users. In order to facilitate interoperability and reusability, HLA differentiates between the simulation functionality provided by the members of the distributed simulation and a set of basic services for data exchange, communication and synchronization.

## 4.2 Architecture and Components

The HLA concept finds a wide applicability through a vast range of simulation application areas such as education, training, analysis, engineering and even entertainment at multiple levels of resolution. These broadly different application areas suggest the variety of requirements that have been taken into account for the development and the ongoing evolution of the HLA standards (IEEE 2000).

Three main components formally define the HLA concept:

- The HLA Framework and Rules Specification summarize a set of rules that en-sure the proper interaction of federates in a federation and define the responsibilities of federates and federations;
- The Object Model Template (OMT) provides the object models that define the information produced or required by a simulation application and for matching definitions among simulations to produce a common data model for mutual interoperation;
- The Federate Interface Specification describes a generic communication interface that allows simulation models to be connected and coordinated, implemented by RTI that will be required for runtime operations.

An HLA ecosystem is divided in its major functional elements, as follows. The first key elements are the simulation resources called federates. A federate can be a computer simulation, an interface to a live system or a support utility such as an event logger or performance monitor. The HLA imposes no constraints on what is represented in a federate or how it is represented, but it does require that all federate incorporate specified capabilities to allow the objects in the simulation to interact with objects in other simulations. These specifications are included into the federation object model (FOM).

The second functional element is the runtime infrastructure (RTI). RTI is a distributed operating system for the HLA ecosystem, and provides a set of general-purpose services that support federate-to-federate interactions, as well as the overall management and support functions.

The third element is the interface to the RTI. The HLA runtime interface specification provides a standard way for federates to interact with the RTI, to invoke the RTI services to support runtime interactions among federates and to respond to requests from the RTI.

The HLA ecosystem defined as above takes the name of HLA federation (Fig. 2) that is a named set of federate applications and a common federation object model (FOM) that are used as a whole to achieve some specific objective. A federation execution is the actual operation, over time, of a set of joined federates that are interconnected through a RTI (Fig. 3).

A detailed discussion of the HLA-based integration between SUMO and Matlab/ Simulink can be found in (Macedo et al. 2013). The integrated platform accounts for the representation of two different systems. On the one hand, there is the traffic system, which are the road network (expressing the physical infrastructure and the topology) and the vehicle-entities that move on it. On the other hand, the electric bus system is defined in terms of its powertrain subsystem such as the set of battery and traction

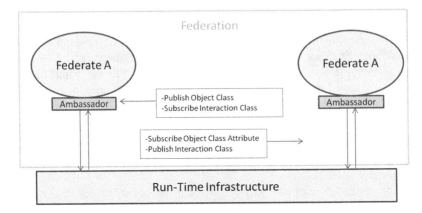

**Fig. 2.** HLA system architecture

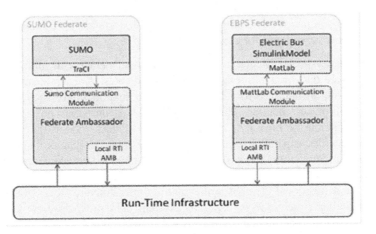

**Fig. 3.** HLA implementation architecture (IEEE 2000)

motor, among others. To address the issues of the traffic system, a microscopic modeling approach is required. The integration among them is achieved by associating the electric bus powertrain subsystem with a vehicle entity (corresponding to a vehicle of class "bus") in the microscopic traffic model.

Thus, important criteria for the selection of the simulators (implementing the microscopic and nanoscopic models) are the ease of access to the respective model variables, the application programming interfaces (API) and communication protocols. In order to implement the physical road infrastructure and the traffic dynamics through vehicular movements in microscopic level resolution, the SUMO software suite has been considered. As for the simulation of electric bus operations and performance, a mathematical model of an electric bus implemented in Simulink has been considered, which represents the main federate components and interactions.

## 5  Simulation Test-Bed

A random route was taken and modeled, considering as base reference the region of Aliados, in the city of Oporto, Portugal. On this route, some bus stops were defined and it was assumed that the bus would stop 20 s at each one of them. Stops at red traffic lights were also considered. In Fig. 4, it can be observed the region of Aliados and a zoom-in on a certain area, where the large green rectangles are bus stops and the smaller yellow one is the bus, stopped at the bus stop (more specifically on the left road segment).

**Table 1.** Acceleration/Deceleration rates for simulation.

| Driver's profile | Acceleration ($m/s^2$) | Deceleration ($m/s^2$) |
|---|---|---|
| Regular | 0.6 | 1.0 |
| Risk taking | 0.9 | 1.0 |

For calculation purposes, it was assumed that the absolute acceleration rates for the risk-taking driver are 50 % higher than rates of regular drivers; the deceleration rate was considered to be the same (Table 1). It is relevant to point out that none of these values surpasses the technical restrictions of the electric bus.

The simulation was then performed twice for exactly the same route: one using regular acceleration rates, based on the normal operation of the bus, and another for the "aggressive" behavior, which for this paper is characterized by higher values of acceleration rates.

**Fig. 4.** Aliados region and detailed representation of traffic on *SUMO* simulator (Color figure online).

## 6 Results

The first analyzed parameter was the amount of energy spent to perform the route. In Fig. 5 it can be seen that the aggressive driver spent 14 % more energy (4.0 kWh) than the regular driver (3.5 kWh) to complete exactly same route.

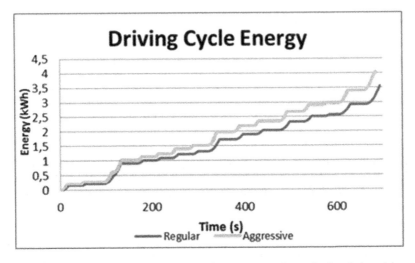

**Fig. 5.** Comparative plot of the amount of energy spent by each electric bus driver.

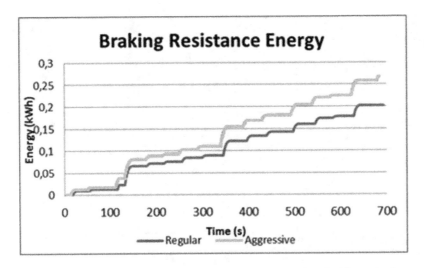

**Fig. 6.** Comparative graph of the amount of energy wasted on braking episodes.

The second analyzed parameter was the amount of energy that is wasted during the braking episodes on the resistance forces to the movement, namely resistance to the air and resistance to the ground. All these forces depend significantly on the speed (indirectly to the acceleration rate), thus it is expected some discrepancy between the outcomes from both driving behaviors.

In Fig. 6, it can be observed that the aggressive driver wastes 0.27 kWh in all braking episodes of this route, while the regular driver spends 32 % less: 0.20 kWh. This parameter is extremely important to calculate the potential to recover energy on braking episodes. Having a risk-taking attitude contributes negatively to this recovery, once this generates a higher boost of energy in such a small period of time (i.e., a braking episode), that batteries would struggle to absorb, due to their low power density (Chu and Braatz 2002).

# 7  Conclusions and Future Work

In conclusion, with this work it became clear how badly driver attitude can affect the energy consumption of an electric bus. Not only is risk-taking behavior dangerous for the driver and the others but it also contributes negatively to an efficient driving performance. In this paper, the case of an electric bus was analyzed and it could be observed that a simple risk-taking attitude, such as accelerating more intensely has a huge influence on the bus performance, either regarding the amount of energy spent to complete a certain cycle, or regarding the potential of energy recovery from the regenerative braking episodes.

Future work encompasses the analysis of other performance parameters, such as the impact of different driving styles on the battery behavior, either regarding its discharging or its ability to charge on braking episodes under those conditions.

Another promising approach to explore in this context is the use of agent-based modeling and simulation, in which autonomous agents would mimic the human reaction to adverse traffic conditions. Agent-based models would thus allow a more detailed analysis of cognitive aspects influencing driver attitude towards more ecologically efficient driving behaviors.

**Acknowledgment.** This work is financially supported by FEDER Funds, through the Operational Programme for Competitiveness Factors – COMPETE under the project grant 13844. Authors acknowledge FCT (Fundação para a Ciência e Tecnologia) support to Deborah Perrotta through PhD scholarship (SFRH/BD/51256/2010) under the scope of the MIT Portugal Program in Engineering Design and Advanced Manufacturing – Leaders for Technical Industries focus area, and to Zafeiris Kokkinogenis through PhD scholarship (SFRH/BD/67202/2009) in the Informatics Engineering doctoral programme at FEUP.

# References

Chu, A., Braatz, P.: Comparison of commercial supercapacitors and high-power lithium-ion batteries for power-assist applications in hybrid electric vehicles I. Initial characterization. J. Power Sources **112**(1), 236–246 (2002). http://linkinghub.elsevier.com/retrieve/pii/S03787 75302003646

Dula, C.S., Ballard, M.E.: Development and evaluation of a measure of dangerous, development and evaluation of a measure of dangerous. J. Appl. Soc. Psychol. **33**(2), 263–282 (2003). http://doi.wiley.com/10.1111/j.1559-1816.2003.tb01896.x. Accessed 25 March 2013

Dula, C.S., Geller, E.S.: Risky aggressive or emotional driving addressing the need for consistent communication in research. J. Saf. Res. **34**(5), 559–566 (2003). http://linkinghub.elsevier.com/retrieve/pii/S002243750300077X. Accessed 18 March 2013

European Union, Summaries for EU Lesgislation (2010). http://europa.eu/legislation_summaries/energy/european_energy_policy/en0008_en.htm

Federal Transit Administration (FTA): Public Transportation's Role in Responding to Climate Change (2010)

IEEE: IEEE Standard for Modeling and Simulation (M & S) High Level Architecture (HLA) — Framework and Rules, pp. 1516–2000 (2000)

Kamal, M., et al.: Development of ecological driving assist system model predictive approach in vehicle control. In: 16th ITS World Congress and Exhibition on Intelligent Transport Systems and Services, Stockholm, pp. 1–11 (2009)

Krajzewicz, D., et al.: Recent Development and applications of SUMO – simulation of Urban MObility. Int. J. Adv. Syst. Meas. **5**(3&4), 128–138 (2012)

Macedo, J., et al.: Electric vehicles Simulink models and SUMO integration: an HLA-based approach of multi-resolution traffic simulation. In: 16th International IEEE Annual Conference on Intelligent Transportation Systems, The Hague, Netherlands (2013)

Miyatake, M.: Theoretical study on eco-driving technique for an electric vehicle considering traffic signals. In: 2011 IEEE Ninth International Conference on Power Electronics and Drive Systems (PEDS), pp. 5–8 (2011)

Perrotta, D., et al.: On the potential of regenerative braking of electric buses as a function of their itinerary. Procedia Soc. Behav. Sci. **54**(2012), 1156–1167 (2012). In 15ª Edition of the European Working Group on Transportation, Paris

# Hybrid Location Management in Vehicular City Environments

Aisling O'Driscoll$^{(\boxtimes)}$ and Dirk Pesch

NIMBUS Centre for Embedded Systems Research,
Cork Institute of Technology (CIT), Cork, Ireland
{aisling.odriscoll,dirk.pesch}@cit.ie

**Abstract.** Unicast geo-routing protocols are reliant on a robust location service protocol to successfully seek the destination vehicle's location. Furthermore successful V2X communication is reliant on the geo-routing protocol to successfully deliver the packet. In both cases successful packet delivery and robustness of the protocols is paramount, the failure of either renders communication a failure. In order to maximise packet delivery, this paper proposes a framework comprised of a location service, the Urban Vehicular Location Service (UVLS), and a geo-routing scheme, the Infrastructure Enhanced Geo-Routing Protocol (IEGRP), that exploits infrastructure where available to function in completely distributed, partially connected and fully infrastructure based networks. Unlike previous protocols that are typically fully distributed or centralised only, the proposed protocols are designed and evaluated to operate in a heterogeneous vehicular environment, specifically to maximise packet delivery and query resolution.

**Keywords:** Location services · Geo-routing · V2X · RSU · Hybrid vehicular networking

## 1 Introduction

There has been a lot of momentum in the Inter-Vehicle Communication (IVC) space in recent years, mainly driven by dedicated spectrum allocation and by the specification of wireless vehicular standards such as 802.11p. Car manufacturers are becoming increasingly interested in a range of applications ranging from infotainment and comfort applications to safety and traffic management. An important aspect of this IVC research, particularly for infotainment applications is to reliably retrieve accurate information relating to vehicle location. This is important from a number of perspectives including service discovery and applications that might be built on top of IVC networks but also from the perspective of getting information to and from vehicles in the network and is achieved using a location service protocol. Vehicular routing is typically based on position based or multi-hop geo-routing protocols and for this you need accurate location information in order for these routing protocols to function correctly. Thus, to route packets in a network it is necessary to identify the location of the destination vehicle.

© Springer-Verlag Berlin Heidelberg 2014
M. Behrisch et al. (Eds.): SUMO 2013, LNCS 8594, pp. 109–135, 2014.
DOI: 10.1007/978-3-662-45079-6_9

However another challenge, is that even once a routing protocol has accurate information, multi-hop routing in a vehicular environment is extremely difficult and it is widely known and documented that reliable multi-hop communications, primarily wide area, cannot be reliably sustained. Road-Side Units (RSUs) can be used to facilitate more reliable communications because they can minimise the need for ad hoc routing and route over a backbone network. Full RSU deployment and coverage may not be available for a considerable period while vehicular infrastructure is being deployed. Thus there is a need for a heterogeneous network, comprising ad hoc and infrastructure components that can scale as the number of RSUs increase.

Thus there is a need to develop a location service and routing protocol that will operate in this heterogeneous environment, exploiting infrastructure where possible to successfully deliver location management and data traffic. These protocols can transition between infrastructureless and infrastructure based networks, generalise well and do not dictate minimum baseline requirements in order to function. This paper thus presents a location management framework by providing a hybrid and robust location service, UVLS and routing protocol, IEGRP, for city and suburban environments.

## 2   Related Work

Current unicast routing algorithms typically provide a completely distributed routing solution or very recently a few authors have proposed centralised only approaches. Distributed vehicular unicast routing protocols can be categorised as position-based [1–10], delay tolerant [11–15] or QoS based [16, 17]. None of these routing protocols consider interaction with partial or full infrastructure, would thus treat a RSU as a "regular" neighbour in the routing algorithm, and will choose a RSU as the forwarding node only if it is the node that makes the greatest greedy progress towards the destination. Furthermore these algorithms are not optimized to prioritize the transmission of packets over a high speed backbone network, rather than via the VANET, if available. Very importantly it should be noted that despite these drawbacks, distributed geo-routing is the defacto routing technique specified in current ITS standards with the GPSR scheme specified as part of the GeoNet project and greedy routing with store and forward buffering specified as part of the ETSI TC ITS reference architecture [18, 19].

Very recently, the benefits of utilising fixed infrastructure as a routing complement to the vehicular ad hoc network, in order to improve reliable end to end multi-hop communications, has been recognised [20–24]. Such schemes typically require dense RSU deployment in prescribed positions as a prerequisite to the correct operation of the routing scheme. This was noted for RAR (start and end of sector) [22], TrafRoute (uniformly distributed with one RSU per sector) [21], ROAMER (widespread deployment) [24] and SADV (every intersection and in the case of partial deployment that they are located uniformly with no backbone connectivity) [23]. Such schemes are thus limited in their generic applicability across a wide range of road topologies that may have restrictions in terms of RSU placement e.g. use of existing infrastructure, or may not lend themselves to uniform deployments. RAR, TrafRoute and ROAMER implement their own proprietary route discovery mechanisms to identify the location of the destination and to establish the route, presenting tightly coupled routing and location service solutions. Packets must follow this pre-determined route towards the destination which is statically determined and does not change, is reassessed at every intersection or the details of how it is determined are unspecified. Importantly, current infrastructure based protocols do not typically specify a recovery mechanism i.e. when a route cannot be found in the ad hoc network before reaching infrastructure or when a RSU does not exist in an expected location. RAR assumes V2I2V with the widespread existence of infrastructure for each sector and does not outline a multi-hop recovery scheme, similar to TrafRoute and Borsetti et al. [20]. SADV assumes RSUs are located at every intersection (though unconnected via a backbone). ROAMER utilizes multicast for redundancy when utilizing ad hoc, V2I or I2V routing, as well as bounded geo-cast communications when in range of the destination node, which incurs high overhead. Vehicular connectivity and widespread RSU coverage is assumed.

Such drawbacks of the current start of the art infrastructure based routing protocols motivates the need for a hybrid routing protocol that can dynamically adapt its routing decisions between distributed and infrastructure based conditions, depending on the network topology under consideration, in order to fulfil the most fundamental of routing objectives - packet delivery. Such a scheme should not dictate the prescribed RSU deployment or density as this does not generalize well and limits its implementation. It should function with any location service protocol that identifies the location of the destination with routing decisions made on a stateless per packet basis, rather than following a pre-determined route.

A plethora of location service protocols have been proposed to date. Majority of these are designed for MANET environments [25–47] and do not cope well with the high dynamism of vehicles and restricted mobility patterns in accordance with the road topology. Distributed vehicular equivalents [48–60] have been proposed but also suffer from limitations, in particular with reduced density, long path lengths and the challenging radio conditions associated with urban vehicular environments. Importantly, they are not equipped to exploit road-side infrastructure if available to maximize delivery of location server packets and also to act as static location servers. Centralised only location services have also been proposed [60, 61] but do not consider partial infrastructure deployment. Many assume the existence of uniformly distributed density of fixed RSUs, located in prescribed locations or it is expected that such RSUs will be located centrally within a partitioned topology that may not comply with the underlying network map [34–37].

Furthermore, many of the current vehicular location service protocols, both distributed and infrastructure-based, have focused on proposing and evaluating the asymptotic costs associated with update and query mechanisms, assuming a node exists in range of a location to act as a distributed server and disregard or do not adequately address the non-uniform disconnected nature of VANETs. Recently, a subset of location service protocols propose aggregated schemes (often hierarchical for locality awareness) to reduce location update and query overhead [35, 36, 55, 56]. This is further in line with the goal of many location services, as already described, to reduce cost of the overhead incurred. Vehicle updates, and in some case query packets, are delayed and aggregated and therefore may experience delay which can lead to reported location inaccuracies. Furthermore all of the afore-described schemes suffer from "service disruption time" (a phrase used in the evaluation of LSVT) [62] i.e. if a vehicle changes cell or group while a location update is occurring, incorrect location information will be returned to a querying location. Lastly a simple technique that would further disseminate vehicle location information is for forwarding vehicles to store 'overheard' location information from packets that it routes. This is currently only considered by one distributed location service protocol, RSLS [58]. The described drawbacks of the current start of the art location service protocols presents the motivation for a location service protocol that can robustly fulfil the most fundamental of location service objectives – location query resolution.

# 3   Urban Vehicular Location Service (UVLS)

The UVLS protocol is proposed to robustly resolve location queries, while maintaining a high query success rate where possible, by increasing access to location servers for update and query procedures. The distinguishing objective of UVLS is that it is focused on delivery and not simply on reducing overhead costs at the expense of successful location resolution or accuracy. This is primarily addressed in its query strategy: which is locality aware while providing functionality to resolve wider area queries.

1. UVLS addresses locality awareness using a road topology aided directional unicast.
2. Wider area queries are resolved by forming a Peer-to-Peer (P2P) overlay network of intersections. As the overlay network is formed of RSUs, no overlay maintenance overhead or inconsistencies arise.
3. Two simple optimization features, location caching/opportunistic query resolution and passive updating are employed to further improve the success rate of the presented location service.

The main components of a location service protocol includes the location server election and maintenance procedure, the location update or registration process (when and how location updates should be disseminated) and the query procedure (how to determine the location server(s) of a destination node given its ID in order to successfully resolve its current location). A description of the UVLS protocol design is now provided to satisfy these criteria, with particular attention paid to the query aspects of the proposed protocol.

## 3.1   UVLS Location Server Management and Registration

In UVLS, static RSUs located at intersections are always favored as location servers. As outlined in the next section, local queries are resolved via a bounded topological unicast so explicit node updates are only required for queries spanning larger areas. Vehicles must firstly determine the frequency with which a vehicle should update its location information. UVLS uses a combination of time and distance based update triggers. Therefore, a vehicle updates when it has travelled a distance that exceeds the distance threshold or based on an expiry timer, whichever occurs first. The timer based update is triggered based on the time taken to travel the distance threshold based on the vehicles average speed.

In UVLS, all RSUs in the vehicular network form a P2P overlay network using the Chord structured Distributed Hash Table (DHT) algorithm [63]. Each RSU hashes its unique identifier to derive its Chord ID, with all Chord IDs forming the overlay ring. As RSUs will remain static and every RSU is aware of the vehicular environment i.e. all other RSUs, bootstrapping and maintenance of the Chord overlay is not a challenge. Each RSU is responsible for a given set of identifiers in the keyspace i.e. vehicle locations in the network. This process is illustrated in Fig. 1, with a vehicle updating the relevant location server.

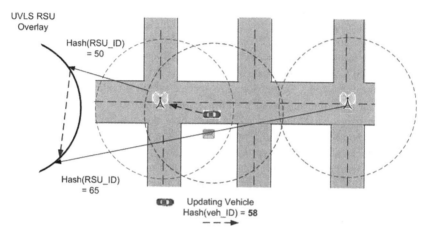

**Fig. 1.** UVLS RSU overlay network

Once a vehicle determines that it must update its location information, it must firstly determine the appropriate location server. In order to do this, UVLS vehicles transmit their location information to the closest intersection with a RSU. As with all forwarding vehicles, the location server at this intersection caches the information in its location table to facilitate fast resolution of local queries. It then determines the vehicle's location server by hashing the unique identifier of the updating vehicle determined via the common SHA-1 hashing function. This location server is the RSU with the closest succeeding ID to the hashed identifier of the updating vehicle. A timer is associated with the update that allows servers to invalidate entries shortly after a new update entry is expected. This timer is calculated based on the current time, the time the update was issued and the speed the vehicle was travelling at the time of issuing the update.

## 3.2    UVLS Location Query Procedure

As previously stated, the goal of UVLS is to prioritise robustness i.e. receipt of location update packets at the correct location server and accurate location resolution. UVLS further addresses locality awareness i.e. where the source and destination vehicles are located in nearby proximity. Thus UVLS is designed to resolve local and wide area location queries and does so by employing a dual approach: firstly seeking the location of the queried destination in the local neighbourhood zone (a geographical area with a bounded Hop Limit (HL) or Lifetime) followed by a wide area search if the location is not resolved. It is envisaged that when the parameters and requirements of vehicular infotainment applications become more clearly defined, that sub-classification of infotainment applications could be identified i.e. whether they are bounded locally or not, in which case UVLS can use one or both of these query mechanisms. In the described protocol implementation, it is assumed that the locality aware query reso-lution approach is first employed, followed by a wider area search if the queried location is not resolved.

To provide locality awareness and resolve local queries, UVLS initially attempts to determine the location of the queried destination vehicle within a five hop perimeter, i.e. the local neighbourhood zone. Five hops has been chosen as this is considered to be the mean upper hop count for successful packet delivery in mobile ad hoc networks [64] and the ETSI C2CNet specification utilises a five HL for its local query resolution. However unlike the ETSI C2CNet location service which broadcasts a packet within five hops, or similar quorum-based location service approaches, UVLS uses unicast packets rather than local broadcasts. This minimises the number of nodes within the local neighbourhood zone that need to be involved in the query or reply process, or involved in the location caching process. Therefore if a source vehicle queries the location of a particular destination node, the query is transmitted as a unicast with each interim forwarding node that receives the query packet looking up its own location database to check whether the queried location can be resolved. If an entry exists, a unicast reply message is generated and transmitted towards the source vehicle, where this location information is used to communicate with the destination. Alternatively if no entry exists in the location database the location query packet is forwarded. The location query is dropped when the HL reaches zero i.e. when it reaches the boundary of the five hop local neighbourhood zone.

Importantly, when the source vehicle initiates the location query, it sets a timeout threshold, the local query timeout, on the transmission of the query. In the case that the local query timeout expires and the source vehicle has not received a location reply packet, it will deduce that the local query has failed and a wide area query is issued. The local query timeout, Ql_timeout (3.1) is derived from the maximum time take to transmit and receive a unicast packet within the HL bounded local neighbourhood zone.

$$Q_{l\_timeout} = \left( \frac{P_{size}}{D_{rate}} + \frac{T_{distance}}{c} + (AIFSN(ac) * T_{slot}) + SIFS \right) * HL \qquad (3.1)$$

where

- $P_{size}$ is the size of a UVLS query packet that is transmitted over the wireless medium, containing the UVLS extensions, ETSI TC ITS and MAC headers. $D_{rate}$ is the network data rate (bps).

- $T_{distance}$ is the propagation distance (m) between the forwarding (transmitting) vehicle and the target destination (receiving) vehicle. As this is not known when estimating the timeout value the maximum radio range is chosen.
- $c$ is the speed of light (3.0E + 08 m/s)
- $AIFSN(ac)$ is the minimum number of slots and is dependent on the specified access category (ac).
- $T_{slot}$ is the duration of the physical layer time slot (13 µs).
- $SIFS$ is the Short Inter-Frame Space, the interval between a data frame and its ACK. This is a constant value of 32 µs.
- $HL$ is the bounded hop limit field specified in the UVLS query packets transmitted within the *local neighborhood zone*.

Another important distinguishing feature of the local UVLS query mechanism, in addition to the use of a unicast, is the consideration of the underlying road topology. As previously stated a bounded geographical area is considered with a HL specified in the location service query packet. However a source or forwarding vehicle located within proximity of an intersection duplicates the query packet as a unicast on all exiting road segments. This is based on the reasonable assumption that vehicles will be enabled with an on-board navigation system and map of the city. Consequently, each vehicle is aware of its current location, the road segment it is on (extracted from the urban map) and whether it is in range of an intersection. The query packet is therefore transmitted in all exiting directions, choosing a point on the road topology exceeding the radio range in order to choose a neighbor to make the greatest greedy progress in the direction specified by the road topology.

If the local query timeout expires without the source vehicle receiving a location reply packet, the source vehicle will next route the query to the location server at the closest intersection with infrastructure. The location server at this intersection will consult its own location database and, assuming that an entry does not exist, will take a particular action depending on the location server type. To facilitate wide area queries, the location server also forwards the updated location information to the closest intersection with a RSU. This RSU forwards the query to the RSU location server at the intersection with the closest succeeding ID determined via the employed Chord common hashing function. UVLS is designed to operate in a partially or fully equipped RSU network. However in an infrastructureless network, it can still function with vehicles at intersections assuming the role of mobile location servers and thus the location service would operate in a flat manner.

The packet delivery rate of UVLS is further improved by two simple optimisation techniques. Firstly, vehicles cache location information that they have passively learned from buffered and forwarded packets. This includes the position vectors of the source vehicle that initiates the UVLS packet but also the position vectors of the interim forwarding nodes. To avoid the situation where stale information is cached and returned to the querying vehicle, a vehicle considers this passive location information to only be valid for a maximum time of t/s, the time it takes a vehicle to exceed the radio range at maximum speed. Thus if a vehicle receives a location query and is not the location server but has an entry stored in their extended location table or determines that it is the destination being queried, it directly sends a location reply to the source vehicle and drops the location query packet. This simple optimization approach improves location service QSR, delays and reduces query path lengths. Furthermore the busier the network becomes i.e. greater dissemination of UVLS updates, queries and replies, leads to greater opportunistic location resolution.

Secondly, a side effect of including the current position vectors of forwarding nodes in UVLS packets is that when a RSU location server receives an update, not only does it initiate the direct update or query process as intended but it updates the relevant RSU location servers (determined by hashing each respective unique vehicle identifier) with this passively acquired information, resulting in accurately stored location information.

In summary, UVLS improves upon current state of the art approaches in a number of ways:

- Many location service protocols are focused on reducing the asymptotic cost of overhead rather than on prioritizing delivery, making false assumptions about connectivity and density. UVLS specifies that RSUs should always be used as static location servers where possible. Once a RSU is reached, the query will be resolved over the backbone network as only intersections containing infrastructure are considered to act as location servers. As an overlay network is employed, the solution is scalable - if a RSU is new deployed in the network, it will be added to the overlay network and the location load redistributed amongst RSUs in the DHT. Furthermore, local queries are resolved via a bounded topological unicast so explicit node updates are only required for queries spanning larger areas.
- Current infrastructure based location service protocols assume full and dense RSU deployment with infrastructure either available at every intersection or more commonly located centrally within an arbitrarily chosen grid. While UVLS makes use of infrastructure, it does not dictate particular RSU placement providing a solution that is more generic in its applicability to a variety of road topologies.
- The use of aggregated update and query mechanisms have also been recently proposed with scheme specific update mechanisms dictating the frequency and operation with which vehicles update their location. While UVLS passively 'aggregates' information by gathering forwarding node's position vectors as the update or query is being routed, it does not delay the forwarding of this information to the relevant location server. Furthermore it achieves greater accuracy due to its location server selection scheme and passive updates. By employing a flat approach, UVLS also does not incur any reported location inaccuracies or overhead due to requirement to re-issue updates when crossing level boundaries as is the case in the afore-described schemes or issues with deploying road topology aware partitioning schemes that may limit its applicability.
- UVLS explicitly considers locality awareness by employing a topologically scoped unicast mechanism so that if a vehicle pair is located in close proximity, the location can be easily resolved. To ensure high delivery, this local query mechanism accounts for the road topology by duplicating the unicast according to the exit mechanism at intersections.

UVLS therefore differs from current state of the art location service protocols in that it does not dictate a mandatory availability or placement of RSU infrastructure, considers locality awareness, prioritizes query resolution and provided accurate location resolution.

# 4    Infrastructure Enhanced Geo-Routing Protocol (IEGRP)

Once the location of a node is determined, routing must be employed for packet delivery. IEGRP is a geographic routing protocol designed to operate over a fully distributed or a partially/fully infrastructure based network and extends our previous work in [65]. Unlike recently proposed infrastructure-reliant approaches described in Sect. 2, it does not demand particular network conditions with respect to RSU availability in order to operate and allows routing algorithms to be dynamically overridden to exploit infrastructure where available.

For fully distributed routing, IEGRP exhibits many characteristics that, in isolation, have been utilised as part of other vehicular routing protocols. A set of generic guidelines for improved VANET routing were recommended in [66] including the use of a store and forward paradigm to cope with temporary disconnections, extended beacon messages (though the content is not specified) and careful selection of forwarding criteria. IEGRP uses store and forwarding buffering to overcome temporary disconnections in the vehicular ad hoc network. Extended beacons are periodically transmitted between one hop neighbour vehicles, including motion and position vectors. The position vector contains the current and previous position of a node, with the motion vector describing a nodes velocity. These extended beacons are used to predict if a vehicle has moved out of the radio range since the timestamp of the last beacon and also to determine the next hop neighbour that will be chosen by the advanced greedy algorithm. In IEGRP, rather than the basic forwarding method of choosing the vehicle that will make the greatest greedy progress towards the destination, IEGRP also accounts for the direction in which the vehicle is travelling and so may choose a vehicle that achieves slightly less progress but is travelling in the direction of the destination. Such an approach has been discussed in the GeoNet final project deliverable [67] as being a possibility for a future extension in the GeoNet specification. In these ways, IEGRP fulfils the optimum criteria for routing in a fully distributed vehicular network. However the primary distinguishing factor of IEGRP is that it exhibits a number of hybrid characteristics, now described and illustrated in Fig. 2:

- IEGRP allows a vehicle's default greedy algorithm to be dynamically over-ridden so that unlike other schemes that choose a neighbour vehicle that makes the greatest geographic distance towards the destination, IEGRP favours a RSU that makes less forward progress to the destination but has a wired link to another RSU that can achieve a greater gain in geographical distance over the infrastructure based backbone. This ultimately offers a better geographical routing gain for packet delivery.
- Similarly, a RSU that may incur a geographic loss in forward progress towards the destination can be chosen if it can route the packet to another RSU geographically closer to the destination over the backbone. Thus in scenarios where the store-and-forward recovery technique would typically buffer a packet, it instead "back-tracks" the packet to a RSU that can route over the backbone.
- RSU neighbours are advertised in periodic vehicle beacons so that indirect neighbour nodes may learn about infrastructure based two hop neighbours. Thus the previous two points consider not only one hop neighbours but also two-hop infrastructure neighbours.

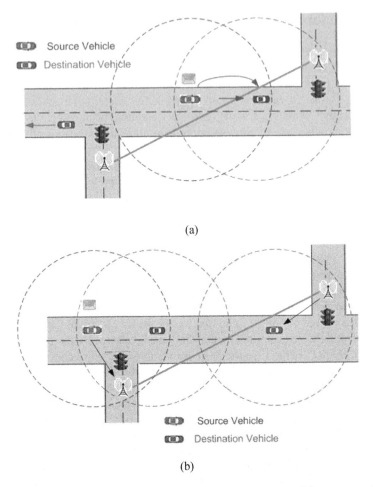

(a)

(b)

**Fig. 2.** IEGRP routing protocol to favour RSU connectivity (a) overriding store and forward mode (b) overriding greedy mode (Color figure online)

In Fig. 2(a), the blue vehicle wishes to route a packet to the red vehicle. As the blue vehicle has reached the local maximum, a geo-routing protocol would ordinarily buffer the packet until a new vehicle is encountered that can make greater geographic progress towards the destination. However IEGRP exploits topology knowledge of RSU neighbours acquired indirectly via two hop beaconing to select an alternative node towards the packet will be forwarded i.e. dynamically overriding the default buffering mechanisms. The routing algorithm operating on the blue vehicle determines that it should multi-hop the packet via the black vehicle to the two-hop RSU. While this will not make a temporary gain towards the destination (it achieves lesser forward progress in the short term), it can route over the wired backbone network (or Internet) to another RSU that will achieve greater physical proximity to the target red vehicle. Similarly in Fig. 2(b), the blue vehicle wishes to route a packet to the red vehicle but the IEGRP routing algorithm will not simply choose the neighbour that achieves the greatest physical progress towards the destination i.e. the black vehicle, as per typical greedy behaviour, but rather forwards the packet to the RSU does not make the best progress to the destination in the short term, but will the best progress to the destination overall.

In contrast to the infrastructure based schemes discussed in Sect. 2, IEGRP does not dictate a mandatory minimum availability of RSUs. Furthermore, it does not require mandatory RSU placement in order to correctly operate (though uniform distribution may improve delivery rates), as it acknowledges that RSUs may be located where there is existing infrastructure and thus it can adapt to varied network topologies. It operates with any location service protocol and most importantly specifies stateless greedy and recovery routing schemes that can dynamically adjust to best accommodate network conditions on a per packet basis to maximise the possibility of packet delivery. This allows IEGRP to adjust dynamically in conjunction with the network topology under consideration.

## 5  IVC Simulation Environment

The performance of UVLS and IEGRP is evaluated using *OPNET*, a commercial network simulator [68] along with the microscopic traffic simulator, *SUMO* [69]. Communication and vehicular traffic parameters are shown in Table 1. A 2500 m × 2500 m Open Street Map (OSM) sub section of Cork City, Ireland, is considered as shown in Fig. 3(a). It is necessary for the OSM map to be manipulated to reflect real vehicular conditions i.e. one way streets, accurate speed limits etc., via Java OSM [70], as shown in Fig. 3(b) with the derived road network subsequently imported into SUMO in Fig. 3 (c). Buildings (polygons) are specified as they are employed in an obstacle model for realistic wireless channel transmission modelling as shown in Fig. 3(d). Varied vehicular traffic densities are generated to model sparse to busy yet free flowing conditions

**Table 1.** IVC simulation parameters

| Parameter | Value |
| --- | --- |
| Simulation duration | 1000 s |
| Application duration | UDP, Exponential (90 s) |
| Number of sender pairs | 10 (constant)- chosen randomly |
| Inter-packet arrival rate | 50 ms |
| Packet payload size | Uniform(100B) with std.dev ± 15B |
| Vehicle densities | $\sim$4–9 veh/km$^2$ |
| Channel model | Sommer et al. obstacle based model with Shadowing + Nakagami small scale fading |
| Maximum transmission range | 210 m |
| Antenna heights | 1.5 m |
| PHY and MAC | 802.11p |
| Beacon interval, timeout | 100 ms, 150 ms |

with vehicles travelling at a maximum speed of 50 kph. The traces are subsequently imported into OPNET as shown in Fig. 3(f). Vehicles are maintained in the network for the duration of the simulation to prevent IEGRP packet loss due to exit of the vehicle. The chosen radio propagation model chosen can have a significant impact on successful packet reception. In this simulation study, an improved version of the Sommer et al. channel model is used [71] that differentiates between Line of Sight (LOS) and Non-LOS between the transceivers utilizing traces of the JOSM buildings. Importantly, the authors of this paper have included small-scale characteristics modelled via the Nakagami-$m$ distribution.

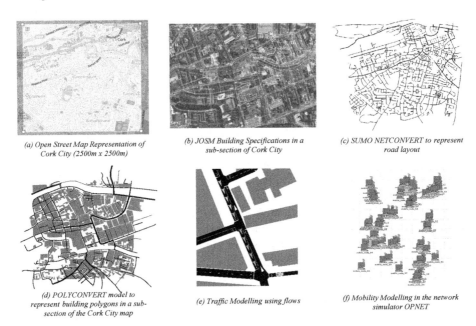

(a) Open Street Map Representation of
Cork City (2500m x 2500m)

(b) JOSM Building Specifications in a
sub-section of Cork City

(c) SUMO NETCONVERT to represent
road layout

(d) POLYCONVERT model to
represent building polygons in a sub-
section of the Cork City map

(e) Traffic Modelling using flows

(f) Mobility Modelling in the network
simulator OPNET

**Fig. 3.** IVC modelling environment

## 6  Performance Evaluation

The performance of UVLS, IEGRP and comparative protocols is evaluated with respect to the following metrics:

*Packet Delivery Rate (PDR):* The PDR is the ratio between the data packets generated at the source vehicle to those successfully delivered to the destination vehicle. An idealised location service is used in the IEGRP evaluation to prevent any protocol unrelated influencing factors.

*Query Success Ratio (QSR):* A query is a lookup made by the routing agent of a node $s$ requesting the location of a node $d$. This excludes queries that $s$ can resolve from its one hop neighbor table. Distinct from the PDR, a query is considered successful if it receives a location reply from the location server that stores $d$'s location information. Therefore the QSR is the ratio of location replies successfully received by source vehicles relative to the overall number of location queries generated. This is evaluated for UVLS only.

*Location Service Accuracy:* The difference in meters between the returned location coordinates relative to the destination vehicle's actual position.

*Location Service Load:* The ratio between all location service control packets transmitted by all vehicles to the total number of replies received i.e. the number of control packets (updates, queries, replies and protocol specific control traffic) required to identify a destination's location.

A prevalent unicast geo-routing protocol has yet to emerge. As such, comparative vehicular routing protocols were chosen in accordance with EU standardisation best practice and specification. IEGRP is compared against C2CNET/GPSR and ISO/ETSI GeoUnicast. *C2CNET/GPSR* [72] specifies the use of the Greedy Perimeter Stateless Routing (GPSR) protocol, utilizing the 'perimeter routing' recovery scheme. *ISO/ETSI GeoUnicast* is specified as part of the ISO/ETSI vehicular communications framework. Its greedy algorithm operates in the same way as that of C2CNET/GPSR but it employs delay tolerant packet buffering. Three IEGRP derivatives are compared, labelled as *IEGRP, IEGRP + OGS (Override Greedy Scheme)* and *IEGRP + ORS (Override Recovery Scheme)*. *IEGRP* does not prioritize infrastructure amongst a vehicle's neighbors however if the default greedy algorithm chooses a RSU as the forwarding node, it ensures that the RSU forwards the packet over the available wired backbone network rather than solely using the wireless VANET. IEGRP + OGS allows the default greedy algorithm to be overridden to favor a RSU one hop neighbor that makes less forward greedy progress can exploit geographical gain over the backbone. IEGRP + ORS allows a temporary geographic loss to occur in favor of infrastructure. V2I schemes, as outlined in Sect. 2, are not directly comparable as they require full infrastructure, often dictating specific RSU locations and a pre-defined route.

UVLS is compared against schemes from each location service including MBLS (hierarchical vehicular scheme) [53], ILS (flat DHT vehicular scheme) [56], C2CNET (a restricted vehicular flooding approach) and GHLS (flat MANET scheme) [62].

## 6.1 UVLS Evaluation

UVLS is evaluated with respect to varied source destination distance ranges. Distance ranges starting at 210m–420m are considered, increasing in 210 m increments (maximum theoretical radio range). The impact of these distance ranges on each location service protocol for 90 vehicles (approximately 5 veh/km) is shown in Fig. 4, which illustrates the mean QSR for a fully infrastructure-equipped network topology and a completely infrastructureless VANET respectively. A low vehicular density has purposely been chosen to emphasize the performance impact of the proposed location service protocol.

It can be observed from Fig. 4(a-b) that across all source distance ranges, for both infrastructure based and infrastructureless scenarios, UVLS outperforms comparative location service schemes to achieve the best QSR. As expected, given the design of UVLS, the QSR is best when infrastructure is available (Fig. 4(a)). What is notable is that UVLS maintains high performance (given the low vehicle density) as distance between the source and destination pairs increases. It maintains performance similar to an idealized location service which will be outlined later in this section. UVLS incurs a 16.37 %, 13.45 %, 42.34 % and 6.25 % increase in QSR when compared with GHLS RR, MBLS, ILS and ETSI TC ITS LS respectively for the 630 m–840 m (approximately 4–6 hop) distance and 10.14 %, 1 % (negligible), 33.03 % and 64.9 % for the 1050 m–1260 m (approximately 6–8 hops) distance. GHLS RR exhibits reduced performance due to the flat nature of the scheme, which is more susceptible to partitions in the network (particular noted in Fig. 4(b)). Secondly, as GHLS was designed for MANETs (yet is frequently used as a baseline comparison) there is a lack of correlation between the location server placement strategy and the underlying topology, causing some hashed server coordinates to be located in areas where there is not a high density of vehicles or even in positions that are not within radio range of the road topology and thus permanently isolated.

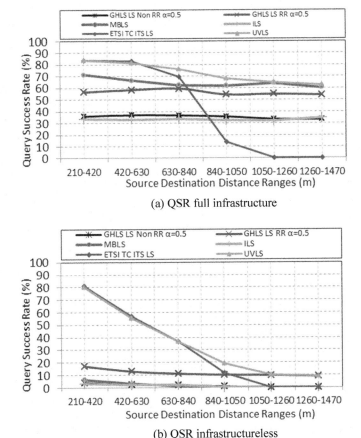

(a) QSR full infrastructure

(b) QSR infrastructureless

**Fig. 4.** Mean QSR for the GHLS, MBLS, ILS, ETSI TC ITS LS and UVLS protocols as a function of varied source destination distance ranges over full infrastructure and an infrastructureless network

It can be noted that *GHLS RR* notes an increase in QSR of when compared to *GHLS Non RR* for the infrastructure based network. Given the frequently disconnected nature of vehicular networks, a forwarding node may consider itself to be the closest node to the hashed location server coordinates, though not within radio range, thereby storing a vehicle's location information and assuming the role of location server. This has a negative impact on protocol performance when a vehicle queries a location to the expected location server coordinates with such queries only resolved if the query packet opportunistically encounters the rogue location server. Thus the improvement noted by *GHLS LS RR* occurs as a result of assuming a DTN approach and buffering updates and query packets until it reaches the closest node with radio range of the coordinates as opposed to the local maximum in the multi-hop network. A number of factors contribute towards declined MBLS performance, even in the case of full infrastructure including its static hierarchical partitioning scheme which is independent of the underlying road topology, reliance on a chain of location servers and its inefficient update mechanism. ILS, as with other schemes performs significantly better when infrastructure is available but is shown to fail completely in an infrastructureless network. This is because the operation of ILS is based on the premise of every intersection in the network becoming part of the P2P overlay network. Given that not every intersection will have a RSU, failure to delivery overlay maintenance packets may lead to inaccuracies and often permanent partitioning of the overlay network i.e. failure of the location service. This is well documented challenge for P2P overlays in mobile networks and one which is exacerbated in high speed vehicular networks [73, 74]. Furthermore, the lack of a timeout policy to phase out stale entries at location servers also impacts accuracy, in turn affecting the PDR. Finally, the ETSI TC ITS LS protocol exhibits comparable performance to UVLS for queried vehicles within the specified 5 hop broadcast limit. This decreases for the 840 m–1050 m scenario for the infrastructure-based scenario. This is to be expected given the broadcast nature of the solution but is at the cost of higher overhead as discussed later. Infrastructure does not impact on ETSI TC ITS LS performance as it is broadcast based. UVLS considers locality awareness similar to ETSI TC ITS LS but also wider area queries by availing of infrastructure located at intersections and the overlay network to maintain consistently high QSR, even with low vehicle density. It does not succumb to the drawbacks associated with the ILS overlay as the DHT ring is formed only of static RSUs connected over a high speed backbone, negating the drawbacks associated with overlay inconsistency. In this way as new RSUs are deployed, they can easily join the overlay network with the location information keyspace redistributed throughout the overlay network. For wider area queries, UVLS is limited only by its ability to multi-hop location updates or queries to the closest RSU i.e. dependent on vehicle density and the availability of infrastructure. Furthermore while ETSI TC ITS LS maintains comparable QSR to UVLS for local queries, UVLS incurs less overhead.

The PDRs incurred by each scheme over a fully infrastructure based and infrastructureless network are shown in Fig. 5(a-b). This is shown as an indication of the accuracy of the locations returned by the location service protocols. It can be noted that UVLS incurs close to perfect PDR (based on an idealized location service) for locality aware queries and out performs all others schemes over increased distance ranges. Importantly, it is acknowledged that the PDR can be impacted by other factors such as availability of a route to the destination and thus no definitive conclusions can be drawn from examining the PDR alone but it is noteworthy to observe that the PDR and QSR for UVLS, GHLS, ETSI TC ITS LS and ILS are very similar. There is greater variation between the QSR and PDR for MBLS.

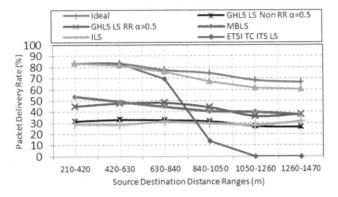

(a) PDR Full Infrastructure

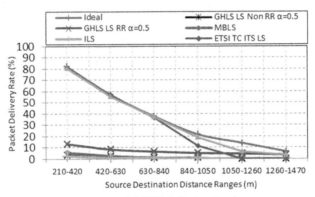

(b) PDR Infrastructureless

**Fig. 5.** Mean PDR for the GHLS, MBLS, ILS, ETSI TC ITS LS and UVLS location service protocols as a function of varied source destination distance ranges over full infrastructure and an infrastructureless network

The performance of the location service protocols are now examined from the perspective of the returned location inaccuracy and overhead incurred. It was noted earlier that the difference between the QSR and the PDR is minor across most schemes as observed in Figs. 4 and 5. This is indicative of little location service inaccuracy, verified in Fig. 6 which shows a CDF of the location error for all location service protocols i.e. the difference between the location of the queried vehicle reported by the location service protocol and its actual location. It can be observed that UVLS, GHLS Non RR and ILS incur small location errors (approximately 80 % of queries are resolved with location errors of 90.9 m, 88.9 m and 95.35 m or less respectively). It must be noted however that while ILS and GHLS Non RR do not incur high inaccuracy, they experience lower QSR than UVLS as previously highlighted. It can be further observed from Fig. 6 that GHLS RR incurs location errors of up to 635 m with MBLS incurring location error of up to 1 km with 86.7 % and 80.2 % respectively of the reported locations under the maximum theoretical radio range of 210 m.

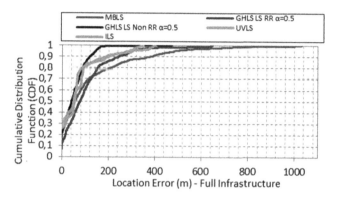

**Fig. 6.** Location Inaccuracy for each location service protocol for 90 vehicles in a full infrastructure based network for the 1050 m–1260 m distance range

ILS updates are based on exceeding the distance threshold with no expiry of the location data at the server i.e. it is simply overwritten by the next more recent update. This leads to the reporting of stale location entries. However the challenges associated with maintaining ILS overlay consistency are so detrimental to performance that this does not cause high inaccuracies in the presented evaluation. GHLS updates are also based on distance but when an update is issued a timeout value is included. The timeout is calculated based on the time taken to move the GHLS distance threshold when travelling at the current speed. If the current speed is zero there is no timeout value placed on the update. As a result this leads to stale entries if a vehicle subsequently updates while moving but this update never reaches the location server. Importantly, as with GHLS, UVLS updates are based on a distance and a timer expiry, whichever occurs first. An expiry of 1.5 times the predicted timeout is used. If a location update with a current speed of 0 is recorded, it is phased out of the location server table after 1.5 times the time it takes to travel the maximum radio range at the maximum speed. Thus, in UVLS, stale entries are timed out at a location server with any inaccurate replies as a result of intolerable delays receiving the location service reply.

However the large location inaccuracies incurred by MBLS are primarily caused by its location update and expiry strategy. When an MBLS location server receives a query, it replies with the predicted location of the vehicle based on its previously stored coordinates and speed as opposed to the actual cached location. In an effort to reduce the location service overhead that is typically associated with periodic updates, a vehicle updates its location only when it passes a new intersection and when crossing a boundary between order squares. This approach decreases the accuracy of the returned location as it does not consider large distances between intersections leading to fewer updates (this is acknowledged by the authors), particularly if subsequent update packets are not successfully delivered. Furthermore the update expiry threshold is calculated as the time taken to travel between intersections in addition to the time taken to travel the radio range at the current speed. Thus if a vehicle updates when moving at a reduced speed or is stopped at an intersection based on a stop sign or traffic light (likely given that MBLS nodes initiate an update packet when at intersections), the timeout associated with the update is very high and does not consider that vehicles do not move at a constant speed.

To summarise, UVLS provides an accurate QSR that out-performs other location service schemes. However, in order to evaluate if this improved QSR is at the expense of a significant increase in overhead, Fig. 7 examines the location service overhead i.e. the number of location service protocol control packets (e.g. updates, query and reply packets) necessary to successfully receive a location service reply. The overhead for

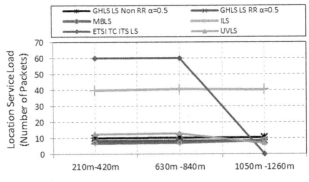

(a) Full Infrastructure (90 vehicles)

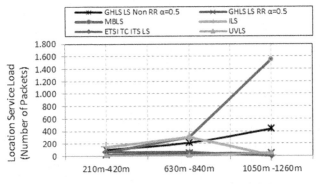

(b) Infrastructureless (90 vehicles)

**Fig. 7.** Location Service (LS) protocol overhead

each location service protocol for the three distance ranges over an infrastructure based and infrastructureless network is considered. Overall it can be observed that, for the most part, all schemes incur similar overhead. Most importantly, UVLS does not incur any significant additional overhead despite improved QSR performance and improved/comparable accuracy. ETSI TC ITS LS incurs the highest overhead for the infrastructure based scenario as it employs a flooding mechanism. ILS also incurs higher overhead than other schemes as a result of overlay stretch. In Fig. 7(b) it can be observed that failure of MBLS to successfully many replies despite transmitting a high number of location service control packets causes significant overhead. A similar situation was noted for ILS though no data point was recorded for ILS for the 1050 m–1260 m distance range as no replies were received and thus the overhead tended toward ∞.

## 6.2 IEGRP Evaluation

IEGRP is evaluated with respect to varied source destination distance ranges and vehicular densities. The impact of these distance ranges on each routing protocol for 520 vehicles (approximately 9 veh/km) is shown in Fig. 8(a-b), which illustrates the mean PDR (standard deviations are negligible) for a fully infrastructure-equipped network and a completely infrastructureless VANET respectively.

It can be observed from Fig. 8 that across all source distance ranges, IEGRP and its derivatives outperform both comparative schemes to achieve the best delivery ratio. As expected, given the design of IEGRP, this is especially the case when infrastructure is available. This improved PDR becomes particularly notable as the distance between the source and destination vehicle increases, with IEGRP derivatives making better use of infrastructure to find a path to the destination. IEGRP + OGS notes an increase in PDR of 34.15 %, 34.35 % and 49.31 % when compared with C2CNET/GPSR (an overall improvement of 67.9 %, 84.73 % and 201 % respectively) for 630 m–840 m (approximately 4–6 hop), 840 m–1050 m (approximately 5–7 hops) and 1050 m–1260 m (approximately 6–8 hops) distance ranges. It incurs an increase in PDR of 20.47 %, 23 % and 39.32 % when compared with ISO/ETSI GeoUnicast (an overall improvement of 31.99 %, 44.32 % and 114 % respectively) over the same distance ranges. This large improvement occurs for two reasons. Firstly, RSUs route packets over the backbone network in order to make greater greedy progress towards the destination vehicle. Secondly, the greedy routing algorithm can be overridden if a RSU is a neighbor as the algorithm recognizes that it may not be located to make the greatest temporary greedy progress in the first instance but can make greater gains over the backbone network with respect to the overall delivery. It can be observed that IEGRP + ORS exhibits a further increase in PDR when compared with IEGRP + OGS of 4.75 %, 5.61 % and 12.16 % for the 630 m–840 m, 840 m–1050 m and 1050 m–1260 m scenarios (an overall improvement of 5.63 %, 7.49 % and 16.48 % respectively). This is because it allows the greedy scheme to be overridden to choose a node that makes a temporary loss in progress but can route closer to the destination over the backbone network. Furthermore IEGRP + ORS incorporates an alternative to the store and forward scheme where packets can be backtracked to a RSU (potentially two hop). In contrast, the delivery rates

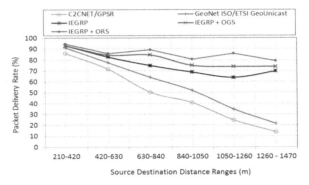

(a)   Fully RSU Equipped

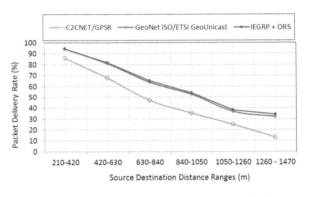

(b)   Infrastructureless

**Fig. 8.** PDR for the C2CNet, ISO/ETSI GeoUnicast, IEGRP, IEGRP + OGS and IEGRP + ORS as a function of varied source destination distance ranges, both (a) with and (b) without infrastructure.

of C2CNET/GPSR and the ISO/ETSI GeoUnicast protocol are highly dependent on the distance between the transmitting and receiving vehicles with an almost linear decrease in successful packet deliveries noted as distance increases, rendering them essentially inoperable. This is mainly as a consequence of increased reliance on multi-hop communications through the VANET which is more susceptible to partitions in the network. The sharp decrease in the performance of C2CNET/GPSR is as a result of its recovery scheme which is not suitable for highly dynamic environment i.e. the challenges in the forming and maintaining a planar graph in vehicular networks, given high vehicle mobility, negatively impacts such a routing scheme leading to routing loops and poor delivery rates. Furthermore, despite the ISO/ETSI scheme employing store and forward buffering and noting an improvement over the face routing recovery scheme of C2CNET/GPSR for all distance ranges, the PDR performance is still highly susceptible to increase in the distance ranges. However IEGRP and its derivatives are not as susceptible to increases in distance range and are relatively distance insensitive as the protocol is designed to exploit infrastructure where possible. It can be noted that IEGRP notes minimal improved delivery rates in the 210 m–420 m (approximately 2–4 hops). The reason for this is the closer proximity between nodes, reducing the likelihood of a preferable path over the wired infrastructure.

Figure 8(b) shows the incurred PDR performance of one of IEGRP's derivatives and comparative routing protocols over a completely infrastructureless network. As the distinguishing factor of IEGRP is that it exploits infrastructure where available, it incurs minor PDR improvements in a completely ad hoc network. However in accordance with the criteria set out in Sect. 3, it employs a greedy scheme (albeit one designed for infrastructure assistance), a store and forward buffering scheme and additional advanced forwarding characteristics in that it selects forwarding vehicles not only based on distance, but also based on their direction of travel in order to maximize delivery. Thus, IEGRP still incurs marginally improved PDR (approximately 3 %) by considering the direction of the next hop mobile neighbor. However, as with all completely distributed routing solutions designed for vehicular networks, it is susceptible to impacted delivery rates when density is decreased and the network is partitioned i.e. when a path does not exist to the destination. In order to evaluate the impact of vehicular density on the routing protocol performance, traffic densities between 4 and 9 vehicles/km were simulated. Thus far, the results discussed in the preceding section assumed 520 vehicles in the network at all times. The performance of the routing protocols as a function of the number of vehicles can be observed in Fig. 9 (a–c). This is graphed across three distance ranges for full infrastructure.

It can be observed that as the vehicle density increases, all protocols experience an increase in the packet delivery ratio. This behavior results from increased network connectivity in the VANET. Overall, it can be observed from Fig. 9 that IEGRP clearly outperforms comparative protocols, demonstrating much improved delivery rates, especially with higher vehicle densities. At lower densities of 90 vehicles, for a distance range of 630 m–840 m, as shown in Fig. 9(b), IEGRP + ORS achieves a PDR of 75.7 %, a considerable increase in the PDR incurred for C2CNET/GPSR (26.98 %) and ISO/ETSI GeoUnicast (41.78 %) as well as the PDR incurred for derivatives of its own scheme, IEGRP (66.1 %) and IEGRP + OGS (66.6 %). As the vehicular density is increased to 520 vehicles, the PDR of IEGRP + ORS grows to 89.19 %, which is an increase in PDR of 38.9 % and 25.22 % over C2CNET/GPSR and ISO/ETSI Geo-Unicast as well as 14.43 % and 4.75 % more than its own derivatives (overall improvement 77.35 %, 39.42 %, 19.3 % and 5.62 % respectively).

When the distance range increases to 1050 m–1260 m, as shown in Fig. 9(a), an increase in vehicular density lends negligible improvement in delivery rates for C2CNET/GPSR and ISO/ETSI GeoUnicast due to the lack of a path through the multi-hop network over a larger distance. Both achieve a PDR of only 9.8 % and 23 % respectively over a 90 vehicle network, increasing to only 24.48 % and 34.47 % respectively for 520 vehicles. For C2CNET/GPSR, these performance issues exist because of the absence of a suitable recovery scheme leaving the protocol susceptible to temporary disconnections in the network. ISO/ETSI GeoUnicast does not suffer degradation for this reason as increased density enables it to overcome voids in the

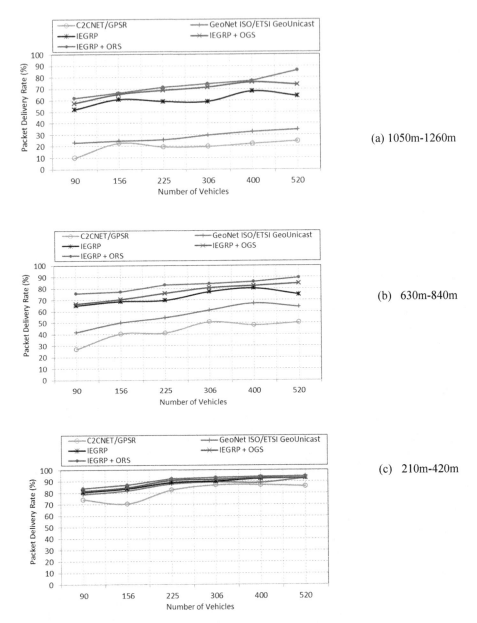

**Fig. 9.** Mean PDR for IEGRP and comparative routing protocols as a function of increasing vehicular density over a variety of source-destination distance ranges

network thereby increasing the likelihood of offloading the packet to a neighbor; however at larger distances this improvement does not sustain adequate delivery rates.

It can be further observed from Fig. 9(c) that IEGRP offers minor performance benefits for the 210 m–420 m distance for the same reasons as outlined in the previous section i.e. proximity of vehicles negating use of infrastructure.

# 7 Conclusion

In this paper a new location management framework for urban vehicular networks is described, comprised of an urban location service, UVLS and an infrastructure enhanced routing protocol, IEGRP. UVLS outperforms current location schemes by employing locality aware and robust query resolution, further enhanced via caching and opportunistic query resolution. To the authors knowledge IEGRP is the first hybrid geo-routing protocol that can adapts its routing decision to transition between distributed, partial and fully infrastructure based networks. While this paper focuses on vehicular location services as a vital prerequisite for geo-routing, this concept is easily transferable to content service discovery which would be useful for implementing publish/subscribe services and content sharing systems.

# References

1. Lochert, C., Hartenstein, H., Tian, J., Fußler, H., Hermann, D., Mauve, M.: A routing strategy for vehicular ad hoc networks in city environments. In: IEEE Intelligent Vehicles Symposium, 9–11 June 2003, pp. 156–161 (2003)
2. Lochert, C., Mauve, M., Fußler, H., Hartenstein, H.: Geographic routing in city scenarios. SIGMOBILE Mob. Comput. Commun. Rev. 9(1), 69–72 (2005)
3. Lee, K.C., Haerri, J., Lee, U., Gerla, M.: Enhanced perimeter routing for geographic forwarding protocols in urban vehicular scenarios. In: Proceedings of IEEE 2007 Globecom Workshops, Washington, USA, November 2007, pp. 1–10 (2007)
4. Seet, B.-C., Liu, G., Lee, F.B.S., Foh, C.-H., Wong, K.-J., Lee, K.-K.: A-STAR: a mobile ad hoc routing strategy for metropolis vehicular communications. In: Mitrou, N.M., Kontovasilis, K., Rouskas, G.N., Iliadis, I., Merakos, L. (eds.) NETWORKING 2004. LNCS, vol. 3042, pp. 989–999. Springer, Heidelberg (2004)
5. Naumov, V., Gross, T.-R.: Connectivity-Aware Routing (CAR) in vehicular ad-hoc networks. In: 26th IEEE International Conference on Computer Communications (INFOCOM), 6–12 May 2007, pp. 1919–1927 (2007)
6. Schnaufer, S., Effelsberg, W: Position-based unicast routing for city scenarios. In: Proceedings of the International Symposium on a World of Wireless, Mobile and Multimedia Networks (WoWMoM 2008), Newport Beach, CA, USA, June 2008, pp. 1–8 (2008)
7. Fußler, H., Hannes, H., Jorg, W., Mauve, M., Wolfgang, E.: Contention-based forwarding for street scenarios. In: Proceedings of the 1st International Workshop in Intelligent Transportation (WIT 2004), Hamburg, Germany, March 2004, pp. 155–160 (2004)
8. Lee, K.-C., Lee, U., Gerla, M.: TO-GO: TOpology-assist Geo-Opportunistic routing in urban vehicular grids. In: Sixth International Conference on Wireless On-Demand Network Systems and Services (WONS), pp. 11–18, 2–4 Feb 2009
9. Lee, K., Le, M, Haerri, J., Gerla, M.: Louvre: landmark overlays for urban vehicular routing environments. In: Proceedings of IEEE WiVeC (2008)
10. Jerbi, M., Senouci, S.M., Meraihi, R., Ghamri-Doudane, Y.: An improved vehicular ad hoc routing protocol for city environments. In: Proceedings of the International Conference on Communications (ICC), Glasgow, Scotland, June 2007, pp. 3972–3979 (2007)
11. LeBrun, J., Chuah, C.N., Ghosal, D., Zhang, M: Knowledge-based opportunistic forwarding in vehicular wireless ad hoc networks. In: IEEE 61st Vehicular Technology Conference (VTC Spring), June 2005, vol. 4, pp. 2289–2293 (2005)

12. Ahmed, S., Kanere, S.S.: Skvr: Scalable knowledge-based routing architecture for public transport networks. In: Proceedings of the 3rd International Workshop on Vehicular Ad Hoc Networks (VANET), pp. 92–93. ACM, New York (2006)

13. Zhao, J., Cao, G.: VADD: vehicle-assisted data delivery in vehicular ad hoc networks. In: 25th IEEE Conference on Computer Communications (INFOCOM), April 2006, pp. 1–12 (2006)

14. Leontiadis, I., Mascolo, C.: GeOpps: geographical opportunistic routing for vehicular networks. In: IEEE International Symposium on a World of Wireless, Mobile and Multimedia Networks (WoWMoM), June 2007

15. Cheng, P.C., Weng, J.T., Tung, L.C., Lee, K.C., Gerla, M., Harri, J.: GeoDTN+NAV: a hybrid geographic and DTN routing with navigation assistance in urban vehicular networks. In: Proceedings of the 1st International Symposium on Vehicular Computing Systems (ISVCS), Dublin, Ireland, July 2008

16. Mo, Z., Zhu, H., Makki, K., Pissinou, N.: MURU: a multi-hop routing protocol for urban vehicular ad hoc networks. In: 3rd Annual International Conference on Mobile and Ubiquitous Systems: Networking and Services, July 2006

17. Namboodiri, V., Gao, L.: Prediction-based routing for vehicular ad hoc networks. IEEE Trans. Veh. Technol. $56(4)$, 2332–2345 (2007)

18. Intelligent Transport Systems (ITS); Vehicular Communications; Part 4: Geographical Addressing and Forwarding for Point-to-Point and Point-to-Multipoint Communications; Sub-part 1: Media-Independent Functionality, ETSI TS 102 636-4-1 V1.1.1 (2011-06), pp. 18, 82, 110, June 2011

19. Intelligent Transportation Systems (ITS); Vehicular Communications; Part 4: Geographical Addressing and Forwarding for Point-to-Point and Point-to-Multipoint Communications; Sub-part 2: Media-Dependent Functionalities for ITS-G5A media, ETSI, work in progress, ETSI-TS-102-636-4-2, pp. 18, 82, May 2010

20. Borsetti, D., Gozalvez, J.: Infrastructure-assisted geo-routing for cooperative vehicular networks. In: IEEE Vehicular Network Conference (2010)

21. Frank, R., Giordano, E., Gerla, M.: TrafRoute: a different approach to routing in vehicular networks. In: VECON, Niagara Falls, Canada (2010)

22. Yanlin, P., Abichar, Z., Chang, J.: Roadside-aided routing in vehicular networks. In: IEEE International Conference on Communications (2006)

23. Ding, Y., Xiao, L.: SADV: static-node-assisted adaptive data dissemination in vehicular networks. IEEE Trans. Veh. Technol. $59(5)$, 2445–2455 (2010)

24. Mershad, K., Artail, H., Gerla, M.: ROAMER: roadside units as message routers in VANETs. Elsevier J. Ad Hoc Netw. (2011). doi:10.1016/j.adhoc.2011.09.001

25. Camp, T., Boleng, J., Wilcox, L.: Location information services in mobile ad hoc networks. In: IEEE International Conference on Communications (ICC) (2001)

26. Basagni, S., Chlamtac, I., Syrotiuk, V., Woodward, B.: A Distance Routing Effect Algorithm for Mobility (DREAM). In: ACM/IEEE International Conference on Mobile Computing and Networking (MobiCom), October 1998

27. Renault, E., Amar, E., Costantini, H., Boumerdassi, S.: Semi-flooding location service. In: IEEE International Conference on Vehicular Technology Fall (VTC), Canada, September 2010

28. Kasemann, M., Fubler, H., Hartenstein, H., Mauve, M.: A reactive location service for mobile ad-hoc networks. Technical Report TR-14-2002, Department of Computer Science, University of Mannheim, November 2002

29. Fan, X., Yang, X., Yu, W., Fu, X.: HLLS: a history information based light location service for MANETs. In: IEEE International Conference on Communications (ICC), South Africa, May 2010

30. Stojmenovic, I.: A scalable quorum based location update scheme for routing in ad hoc wireless networks. Technical Report TR-99-09, SITE, University of Ottawa, September 1999

31. Jiang, J.-R., Ling, W.-J.: SEEKER: an adaptive and scalable location service for mobile ad hoc networks. In: ACM International Conference on Supercomputing (ICS), Italy, June 2006

32. Bae, I.-H.: An adaptive location service on the basis of diamond quorum for MANETs. In: IEEE International Conference on Natural Computation (ICNC) (2007)

33. Abraham, I., Dolev, D., Malkhi, D.: LLS: a locality aware location service for mobile ad hoc networks. In: 2004 Joint Workshop on Foundations of Mobile Computing (DIALMPOM) (2004)

34. Chang, G.-Y., Sheu, J.-P.: A region-based hierarchical location service with road adapted grids for vehicular networks. In: 39th IEEE International Conference on Parallel Processing Workshops (ICPPW), San Diego, USA, September 2010

35. Saleet, H., Basir, O., Langar, R., Boutaba, R.: Region-based location-service-management protocol for VANETs. IEEE Trans. Veh. Technol. **59**(2), 917–931 (2010)

36. Woo, H., Lee, M.: Mobile group based location service management for vehicular ad-hoc networks. In: IEEE International Conference on Communications (ICC), Japan, June 2011

37. Li, J., Jannotti, J., De Couto, D.S.J., Karger, D.R., Morris, R.: A scalable location service for geographic ad hoc routing. In: International Conference on Mobile Computing and Networking (MobiCom), USA, August 2000

38. Xue, Y., Li, B., Nahrstedt, K.: A scalable location management scheme in mobile ad-hoc networks. In: IEEE Conference on Local Computer Networks(LCN), November 2001

39. Kieß, W., Füßler, H., Widmer, J.: Hierarchical location service for mobile ad-hoc networks. ACM SIGMOBILE Mob. Comput. Commun. Rev. **8**, 47–58 (2004)

40. Yu, Y., Lu, G.-H., Zhang, Z.: Enhancing location service scalability with HIGH-GRADE. In: IEEE International Conference on Mobile Ad-Hoc and Sensor Systems (2004)

41. Cheng, T., Lemberg, H.-L., Philip, S.-J., Van den Berg, E., Zhang, T.: SLALoM: a scalable location management scheme for large mobile ad-hoc networks. In: IEEE WCNC, March 2002

42. Seet, B.-C., Pan, Y., Hsu, W.-J., Lau, C.-T.: Multi-home region location service for wireless ad hoc networks: an adaptive demand driven approach. In: WONS (2005)

43. Das, S.-M., Pucha, H., Hu, Y.-C.: On the scalability of rendezvous-based location services for geographic wireless ad-hoc routing. Elsevier Comput. Netw. **51**(13), 3693–3714 (2007)

44. Woo, S.-C., Singh, S.: Scalable routing protocol for ad hoc networks. Wirel. Netw. **7**(5), 513–529 (2001)

45. Wu, X.: VDPS: virtual home region based distributed position service in mobile ad hoc networks. In: IEEE International Conference on Distributed Computing Systems (ICDCS), USA, June 2005

46. Cheng, H., Cao, J., Chen, H.-H., Zhang, H.: GrLS: group-based location service in mobile ad hoc networks. IEEE Trans. Veh. Technol. **57**(6), 3693–3707 (2008)

47. Rao, R., Liang, S., You, J.: LBLS: a locality bounded hashing-based location service. J. Netw. **5**(1), 19–27 (2010)

48. Geonet project: http://www.geonet-project.eu. Final Specification, January 2010

49. Ahmed, S., Karmakar, G.-C., Kamruzzaman, J.: Hierarchical adaptive location service protocol for mobile ad hoc networks. In: IEEE International Conference on Wireless Communications and Networking (WCNC), Hungary, April 2009

50. Flury, R., Wattenhofer, R.: MLS: an efficient location service for mobile ad hoc networks. In: ACM International Symposium on Mobile Ad Hoc Networking and Computing, Florence, Italy, May 2006

51. Wang, W., Chinya, V., Ravishankar, V.: Hash-based virtual hierarchies for scalable location service in mobile ad-hoc networks. Mob. Netw. Appl. **14**, 625–637 (2009)
52. Bae, I.-H., Kim, Y.-J.: An adaptive location service on the basis of fuzzy logic for MANETs. In: IFSA World Congress, Theme: Theory and Applications of Fuzzy Logic and Soft Computing, Mexico, July 2007
53. Boussedjra, M., Mouzna, J., Bangera, P., Manohara Pai, M.M.: Map-based location service for VANET. In: IEEE International Conference on Ultra Modern Telecommunications and Workshops (ICUMT), St. Petersburg (2009)
54. Brahmi, N., Boussedjra, M., Mouzna, J., Cornelio, A.K.V., Manohara Pai, M.M.: An improved map-based location service for vehicular ad hoc networks. In: IEEE International Conference on Wireless and Mobile Computing, Networking and Communications (WiCOM), China, September (2010)
55. Ashok, D.M., Manohara Pai, M.M., Mouzna, J.: Efficient map-based location service for VANETs. In: IEEE International Conference on ITS Telecommunications (ITST), Russia, August 2011
56. Chang, Y.C., Shih, T.L.: Intersection location service and performance comparison of three location service algorithms for vehicular ad hoc networks in city environments. In: IEEE International Symposium on Wireless Pervasive Computing (ISWPC), Greece, May 2008
57. Xiang-yu, B., Xin-ming, Y, Jun, L., Hai, J.: VLS: a map-based vehicle location service for city environments. In: IEEE International Conference on Communications (ICC), ICC '09 (2009)
58. Zhang, G., Chen, W., Hong, L., Mu, D.: A novel location service for urban vehicular ad hoc networks. In: IEEE International Symposium on Microwave, Antenna Propagation and EMC Technologies for Wireless Communications (2009)
59. Zaki, S.M., Ngadi, M.A., Razak, S.A., Kamat, M., Shariff, J.M.: Location service management protocol for vehicular ad hoc network urban environment. In: Meghanathan, N., Chaki, N., Nagamalai, D. (eds.) CCSIT 2012, Part II. LNICST, vol. 85, pp. 563–574. Springer, Heidelberg (2012)
60. Hosseininezhad, S., Leung, V.: Reliability-based server selection for heterogeneous VANETs. ICST Trans. Mob. Commun. Appl. **11**(7–9) (2011). http://eudl.eu/doi/10.4108/icst.trans.mca.2011.e4
61. Gerla, M., Lee, U., Zhou, B., Lee, Y., Marfia, G., Soldo, F.: Vehicular grid communications: the role of the internet infrastructure. ACM International Workshop on Wireless Internet (WICON'06), USA, August 2006
62. Woo, H., Lee, M.: Vehicle location service scheme using the vehicle trajectory for VANETs. In: IEEE International Conference on Advanced Communications Technology (ICACT), Korea, February 2012
63. Stoica, I., Morris, R., Karger, D., Kaashoek, M.F., Balakrishnan, H.: Chord: a scalable peer-to-peer lookup service for internet applications. ACM SIGCOMM Comput. Commun. Rev. **31**, 149–160 (2001)
64. Tseng, Y.-C., Li, Y.-F., Chang, Y.-C.: On route lifetime in multihop mobile ad hoc networks. IEEE Trans. Mob. Comput. **2**(4), 366–376 (2003)
65. O' Driscoll, A., Pesch, D.: An infrastructure enhanced geographic routing protocol for urban vehicular environments. In: IEEE Wireless Vehicular Communications (WiVec), Dresden, Germany, June 2013
66. Cabrera, V., Ros, F.J., Ruiz, P.M.: Simulation-based study of common routing issues in VANET routing protocols. In: IEEE Vehicular Technology Conference (VTC), Barcelona, April 2009
67. GeoNet: D2.2 Final GeoNet Specification. Public deliverable, pp. 77, 101, June 2010
68. OPNET network simulator. http://www.opnet.com

69. Behrisch, M., Bieker, L., Erdmann, J., Krajzewicz, D.: SUMO - Simulation of Urban MObility: an overview. In: SIMUL 2011, The Third International Conference on Advances in System Simulation, pp. 63–68 (2011)
70. http://josm.openstreetmap.de/
71. Sommer, C., Eckhoff, D., German, R., Dressler, F.: A computationally inexpensive empirical model of IEEE 802.11p radio shadowing in urban environments. In: Conference on Wireless On-Demand Network Systems and Services (WONS), January 2011
72. Car-to-Car Communication Consortium Manifesto (Overview of the C2C-CC System), pp. 14, 20, 24, 25, August 2007
73. Liu, C., Wang, C., Wei, H.: Cross-layer mobile chord P2P protocol design for VANET. ACM. Int. J. Ad Hoc Ubiquitous Comput. **6**(3), 150–163 (2010)
74. Heer, T., Gotz, S., Rieche, S., Wehrle, K.: Adapting distributed hash tables for mobile ad hoc networks. In: IEEE International Conference on Pervasive Computing and Communications Workshops (PERCOMMW), Pisa, Italy, March 2006

# Real-Time Simulations Based on Live Detector Data – Experiences of Using SUMO in a Traffic Management System

Mario Krumnow[(⊠)] and Andreas Kretschmer

Chair of Traffic Control Systems and Process Automation,
Dresden University of Technology, Andreas-Schubert-Str. 23,
01069 Dresden, Germany
{mario.krumnow,andreas.kretschmer}@tu-dresden.de

**Abstract.** An accurate real-time simulation of traffic behaviour requires a large amount of very specific data. It seems obvious that the use of currently measured data from the field is a great opportunity to lead a simulation as close to reality as possible. Once a realistic simulation of the traffic behaviour is available, many applications are imaginable. It is possible to simulate different scenarios to support the decision making process. Forecasts of the impacts of different management strategies can be analyzed fast and easily to help improving the quality of urban traffic. Furthermore a prediction of future traffic states can be made using currently measured data of the traffic situation.

**Keywords:** Microscopic traffic simulation · Traffic management · VAMOS · Dresden

## 1 Motivation

In the city of Dresden the regularly operated Traffic Management System VAMOS combines data from various traffic data sources, which provide information about the past and current traffic situation [2]. Data from sensors and actuators can be used to feed and calibrate the micro simulation. Most of the data is collected by induction loops, which measure the traffic volume as well as the composition of traffic. Further sources for collecting traffic data are floating cars, which provide information about their own position and velocity. Recently gathered online data from actuators like traffic lights, variable message signs and variable traffic control units may also be used to feed the simulation. In consideration of the mentioned online traffic-data simulation tools like SUMO can be used to determine traffic situations for several parts of a traffic system, dedicated for different modes of transport (such as private traffic or public transport) as well as for the whole overall transportation system [1]. To have a simulation suite under the terms of a General Public License is a main requirement. It offers transparency issues like the possibility to look in the code. Another important fact is the right to change the software to fits perfectly our needs. The simulation should be very fast to simulate a given scenario faster than real-time to have real benefit. In SUMO there is a special binary which offers the possibility to run simulation in a

© Springer-Verlag Berlin Heidelberg 2014
M. Behrisch et al. (Eds.): SUMO 2013, LNCS 8594, pp. 136–145, 2014.
DOI: 10.1007/978-3-662-45079-6_10

headless mode. That saves a lot of time because of the missing rendering time for the user interface.

Altogether simulation assisted calculation might ease or even enable the estimation of traffic states for complex transport networks and at least help to improve forecast quality.

## 2  Data Sources

Data from various sources like detectors or actors are collected and processed by the basic services of the management system VAMOS. Those data is transmit over various physical interfaces e.g. copper, optical fiber or wireless. Each detector can have there on physical address and data protocol so this is a very heterogeneous field in traffic science. One task of VAMOS is the conversion of the received data into well-known data formats to store it in several relational databases. For some detectors even a continuous data stream is available, e.g. cameras or automatic traffic counters. That kind of data is stored into memory caches and periodically transmit into database tables. That means the information is available in the moment it is received but there is some delay before it is stored in the database.

In cases of traffic micro simulations the clue is to send the collected informations directly to it that means there is only very small time delay between the real measured event in the field and the event in the simulation [3]. The next section will give a small overview about the available traffic data sources and how to use them in a micro simulation.

### 2.1  Traffic Volumes

For the whole city of Dresden an up-to-date traffic volume map is available which represents information about the daily traffic volume and the percentage of heavy traffic (Fig. 1) [4]. The traffic volume map provides no further information about the classification of the traffic volume into specific classes like cars, motorbikes or trucks. Though, that information is important for the calibration of the simulation and for reliable statements concerning the emission and the average speed in the SUMO network model.

Moreover, the traffic volume map contains no information about the distribution of traffic at intersections. For that reason the traffic surveys are carried out periodically to determine these distribution values. The information about the current traffic load is gathered by automatic traffic counters which can also be used to get knowledge about the traffic distribution.

### 2.2  Traffic Lights

To model the behavior of the traffic light control it is necessary to correctly reproduce the TLS program. Due to the fact that traffic light signaling differs in kind of control – especially regarding the degree of dependency on traffic situation and data – several approaches covering different cases have to be considered.

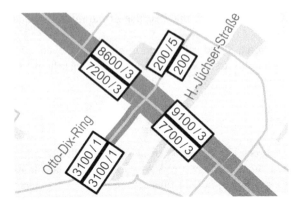

**Fig. 1.** Part of a traffic volume map (format: daily traffic/percentage of heavy traffic)

The simplest case is a fixed time control. Here the main task is to define the switching times for each signal group. This is typically done in TLS cycles where the initial timestamp of the first cycle has to be valid so that there is no offset to the TLS outside in the field. The more sophisticated case is the traffic actuated TLS control whereas dynamic cycle times and traffic influenced green phases exists. Besides the dependency on data about private traffic, controlling is particularly affected by input from and about public transport and has therefore to be considered for reproduction. For example, in Dresden more than 80 % of the TLS have the opportunity to interact with the public transport. At the moment the implementation of traffic actuated signal controls in SUMO is a complex and very time consuming process. The whole TLS logic has to be implemented in SUMO because tools to import native TLS programs, e.g. VS-PLUS are not yet available.

One approach to integrate the input values for the TLS control is the usage of induction loops within the simulation. The data is then pushed to the TLS software control influencing the simulated TLS. Another approach is to build up a hardware-in-the-loop model. In this case an existing TLS hardware controller would be needed to put the data from the simulation to the controller input unit. The hardware controller generates signals for the TLS controlling which are pushed back from the controller output unit to the simulation.

Both variants are not useful for huge networks, because all current TLS algorithms have to be implemented either as part of the simulation or as specific model. Even the detailed maps including detector locations have to be reviewed and to be integrated into the simulation. Whilst execution of a simulation each single detector measuring value has to be transferred in real time to be considered within this simulation cycle. That means that various kinds of detectors like induction loops, cameras, traffic eye universals etc. have to be imported and calibrated correctly. A decision has to be generated whether the detector works properly and no systematic failures (like interchanged channel numbers for single induction loops) exist. Altogether, both approaches might lead to highly accurate simulation, but are nevertheless not or hardly affordable.

Highest priority was given to the simulation of a traffic network rather than one more exact copy of one single TLS controller. Thus, and because of the expected affords for the both approaches described above, another opportunity was taken into account. The third approach is to capture only the exact signal states of the TLS controller in the field and push them to the TLS in the simulation to override the state of the default traffic signal control. In comparison to the previously described approaches the third one demands a trustworthy simulation. This means the traffic volume and all the physical parameters have to match precisely with the reality which is hardly to achieve. In order to forecast the future signal states some algorithms for traffic actuated controllers have been developed [7]. This information will also be pushed to the TLS control in the simulation to get some information for some decision making processes.

### 2.3   Floating Car Data

In Dresden a fleet of 500 taxis collects floating car data. Position, velocity and an occupied flag are recorded every 5 s. These data are used to determine the level of service (LOS) for all parts of the entire traffic network. Several algorithms integrated in VAMOS verify the generated LOS messages by comparing the FCD message with other traffic detectors like automatic traffic counters [2].

Moreover, it is possible to generate highly accurate maps of the entire traffic network. This depends on the accuracy of the GPS location and the frequency of the GPS tracker signal. In Fig. 2 the GPS location points are connected so that a map becomes visible.

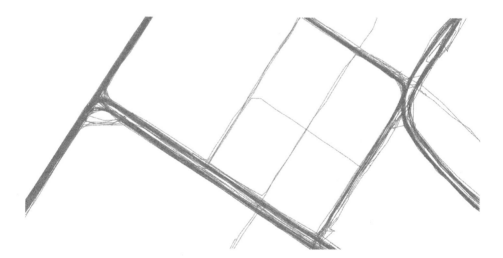

**Fig. 2.** Generated map based on floating car data

These taxi FCD data can be used to validate the simulation findings. In cases of inaccuracy within the simulated scenario the velocity can be adjusted to a lower or even a higher value. Consequently vehicles on a specific link will be removed to dissolve traffic jams. Additionally the FCD data are suitable to decide whether the simulated traffic works well or not.

These data can also be used to calibrate the driver model used by the simulation. This can be done by analyzing the raw input material and as a result of a data fusion with other data sources, e.g. traffic lights or traffic counters. So the values for car following models like the Krauss model can be obtained.

## 2.4  Public Transport Data

In Dresden most of the TLS are influenced by public transport. In order to reproduce a realistic behaviour of the public transport vehicles routes for busses and trams are specified. Subways or light rails were not modelled because they do not interact with the individual traffic on the roads.

The simplest approach is to use a fixed time schedule (accurate to a minute) for public transport representing realistic traffic behaviour in a rough manner only. For higher accuracy more information is needed, initially static information as the planned arrival time (accurate to a second), detailed information about the speed profile of the vehicles or the speed restrictions in front of curves or at tram switches.

Also information about the current location in association to the positions according to the time schedule and the dwell time at the stops are necessary. For that purpose the data of a special measuring tram which is part of the cooperation between public transport operators and the Dresden University of Technology can be accessed. Additionally information results from corresponding probes gathered for bus and again tram lines with a mobile GPS logger. In summary, the first approach seems to be very rough, but allows gaining information for a whole network with less afford. The comparison to data of the additional information sources mentioned above results in good average quality and accuracy for public transport in Dresden. However, users have to consider that quality gathered according to the method of this first approach may depend on the operational and quality management of the public transport aiming to keep close to their time schedule. In case of special situations and therefore as requirement for high quality traffic and transport management this approach might not be suitable without restrictions.

According to the tasks in traffic management (e.g. management in case of large-scale events and in case of incidents relevant to the transport network) and as a base for high quality management the second approach deals with more situation depending data. As additional input real time data from the local transport company (Dresdner Verkehrsbetriebe) is available. This data is generated by an intermodal transport control system (ITCS) which is based on an analogue radio system. By using a pull mechanism the position of each bus and tram is captured every 15 s.

With this data more accurate information about the arrival and leaving times at the stops is available. Furthermore incidents or the location of transfer synchronization points can be identified. In a first implementation properties of both approaches have been considered and integrated: Trams as well as busses are put into the simulation at a specific time but already based on the information on the telegrams of the ITCS. In future work the position of the public transport will be also controlled for the whole route by moving or teleporting forward or backward on the route. Also the routes of the public transport should be able to be adapted because of special events like returning to the depot or because of incidents in the network.

## 2.5   Parking Data

The information about the current load of parking lots in the city is available. The management system also predicts a trend of the load for the next couple of minutes. At the moment this data is not used because of the unnecessary parking events within the simulation. Nevertheless this kind of data might be used in the future to simulate a more realistic driver behavior which is based on dynamic data.

Another fact is a specific feature of the local Parking guidance systems of Dresden. With use of a movable arrow the traffic can be influenced to use a strategic route to the parking lots. The position of that arrow is controlled by the traffic management centre that means the information is available and can be used for the simulation. The routes of the traffic flow are calibrated with that data.

## 2.6   Rerouting Systems

To advise drivers of alternative routes over fifty variable message signs were installed all over the cities road network. (Fig. 3) That signs are controlled by the traffic management system in order to react on incidents in the traffic flow. The decision to use a specific road to a defined location is taken by implemented algorithms. The main idea is to route the traffic strategically through the network to avoid traffic jams. Those route decisions can be different from the routing algorithms of the individual navigation devices of the drivers. This is because of the global optimization criteria of the algorithm. On the other hand some traffic forecast information is available which is unknown to the navigation device.

In the simulation the data is used to reroute the existing vehicles respectively to use the routes for new vehicles.

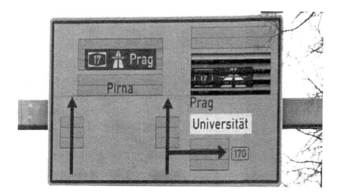

**Fig. 3.** Variable message sign to advise drivers of alternative routes

### 2.7  Camera Data

A lot of cameras distributed all over the city can be accessed by the management system. Most of the cameras are installed at the traffic lights to work as an optical detector for the TLS control. The video data will be used to validate the simulation results. Due to the lack of tools for automated integration and as the process for calibration of the image recognition is very time consuming, this validation is done in a manual way as a first step.

In the future important image recognition algorithms for cameras exclusively driven for traffic management might be calibrated for example to compare the current queue length with the queue length in the simulation. The concept here is to compare the queue tail of the simulation with the queue tail at the same time within the camera image.

## 3  Real Time Simulation Setup

### 3.1  Building the Network

SUMO has already a tool to import OpenStreetMap (OSM) data, which is not suitable for the road network of Dresden. Reasons are the low level of detail within the generated SUMO network, incorrect numbers of lanes per road section and incomplete information about primary and secondary roads. Finally, the existing net model of the traffic management system VAMOS was used as the base for a SUMO network. That model is mapped in a MySQL database where the geometries of all elements are stored in different tables. The VAMOS network model includes information about the geometry of each lane, the edges and the intersections. Also the connections between the lanes are available.

The task was to build SUMO shapes from the VAMOS geometries and import the information about the connections between the edges. Because of the XML exchange format of the SUMO net file, this task can be reduced to a simple conversion between both data sources. The use of geometric simplify algorithms like the Ramer–Douglas–Peucker algorithm is useful because the resulting simulation does not need such a high accuracy for computation.

### 3.2  Access the Simulation

To handle and simplify the integration of several and different data sources a universal interface is needed which can be accessed by several applications like the modules for handling the detector data [8]. Another requirement is that the simulation should act as a service which means that the simulation will not terminate to a specific time. A suitable solution is a web service that interacts with SUMO and handles all connections to the several clients. This service (TraCI as a service – TraaS) was fully implemented in Java and is available on OpenSource Website. It is also available in the contributed section of the current SUMO Release 0.19.0 The *TraaS* web service uses the well-known Simple object access protocol (SOAP) instead of the TraCI byte code and is based on a TCP/IP connection.

In Fig. 4 the concept of the Web Service is shown. On the left side all input values are pushed to the service and will then be forwarded to different instances of SUMO. Those instance can represent different scenarios and forecast levels. It is easy to scale up that process by adding more servers to the system or use concepts of cloud computing.

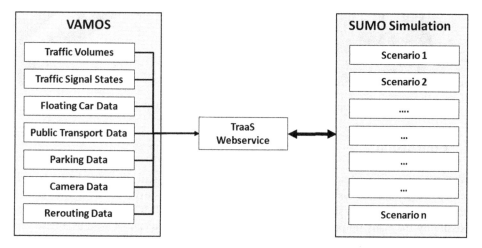

**Fig. 4.** System setup to interact with different instances of SUMO

## 4  First Results

In a first realistic simulation an arterial of Dresden including 15 traffic signals with individual traffic as well as public transport vehicles was modelled [5]. By the help of this model the advantages of the real-time I/O data interface are demonstrated. Other works [6] dealt with the simulation of a single intersection, concentrating on the emission output of vehicles depending on the traffic signal program. As measuring emissions in practice is a real challenge, it is very helpful to have a simulation-based assessment in order to choose the best suiting signal program to reduce these emissions. An analysis of congestions in front of intersections, depending on the traffic signal program, has also been carried out. Figure 4 shows, that video images and snapshots from the simulation can be compared to verify congestions at an intersection.

Most of the gathered test series seem to have sufficient quality in representing the real traffic situations and passed cursory plausibility tests. In Fig. 5 a comparison of the simulated velocity and the real velocity of a taxi is shown. The route has a length of approximately 9 km and various traffic adapted signal lights. At two discrete locations the traffic volume is measured with automatic traffic counters. The behaviour of the taxi driver in adapting the velocity is smoother. The opportunity to choose the maximum acceleration or deceleration of the vehicle is not used so often in the real taxi because of the forward-thinking behaviour of the driver. This driving style is also more comfortable for the passengers.

**Fig. 5.** Comparison between video image and simulation snapshot

## 5 Conclusion

With the approaches described a first implementation of a real-time simulation based on live detector data has been developed and tested. The developed real-time simulations of specific traffic situations can be processed with SUMO very fast and offer the possibility for many output options. This various output data can be used as a base for extensive subsequent analytical processes. In order to predict the reaction of traffic participants on the applied strategy, many simulations can be run in a parallel mode.

According to the positive first results and the benefits seen in additional simulations one of the next steps should be the thoroughly analysis of data quality which can be achieved by using SUMO real time simulation. For further use in daily operation users and developers should be aware that data quality can be assumed as sufficient only while measuring and passing comparison to detailed data of the real traffic network. For that reason additional future tasks would be the definition of an initial calibration process and for the ongoing quality management based on supporting points.

Using live detector data in SUMO at least offers numerous possibilities for traffic analysis and, by the help of comparison, for the further development of the simulation software itself. A further main aspect is the supported replication of the current traffic situations by the simulation. Starting from that view it is particularly interesting to compare the progresses within the real traffic network with the one in the simulation environment. With the implementation and testing of real time simulation an essential pre-condition for the application SUMO for a variety of new tasks and especially for its integration into short term decision making processes has been carried out.

In particular, the potential for testing traffic management measures before applying them to the field actuators and mainly the opportunity to analyze more than one single traffic measure or more than one single strategy simultaneously or almost in real time let expect new and important findings.

Currently Research engineers and students of the Dresden University of Technology are working constantly on the improvement of that kind of real-time simulations to ensure the quality and represent the reality as accurate as necessary.

# References

1. SUMO – Simulation of Urban Mobility (2012). Institute of Transportation Systems, German Aerospace Center, Germany. http://sumo-sim.org. Accessed 12 December 2013
2. VAMOS - Verkehrs-Analyse-, Management- und Optimierungs-System (2012). Chair of Traffic Control Systems and Process Automation, Dresden University of Technology, Germany. http://www.vamosportal.de. Accessed 12 December 2013
3. Microscopic real-time simulation of Dresden using data from the traffic management system VAMOS, 19th ITS World Congress Vienna, Austria, 25 October 2012
4. http://www.dresden.de/de/08/02/publikationen/003_Verkehrsmengenkarte.php. Accessed 12 December 2013
5. Arlt, A.: Realitätsnahe Simulation des Verkehrsflusses auf der Süd-West-Umfahrung in Dresden mit SUMO unter Berücksichtigung des MIV und des ÖPNV (in German). Report student research project, Dresden University of Technology, Germany (2012)
6. Reiche, M.: Vorher-Nachher-Analyse der Emissionsbelastung am Knotenpunkt Nürnberger Platz im Rahmen der ÖPNV-Bevorrechtigung des NSV-Projektes (in German). Report student research project, Dresden University of Technology, Germany (2012)
7. Krumnow, M: Schaltzeitprognose verkehrsadaptiver Lichtsignalanlagen im Rahmen des Projektes EFA 2014/2, 8. VIMOS Konferenz, Dresden (2012)
8. Krumnow, M,: Verkehrsmikrosimulationen mit Echtzeitdaten – Herausforderungen und Chancen, 9. VIMOS Tagung, Dresden (2013)

# Real-Time Traffic Conditions with SUMO for ITS Austria West

Karl-Heinz Kastner, Robert Keber, Petru Pau$^{(\boxtimes)}$, and Martin Samal

RISC Software GmbH, Softwarepark 35, 4232 Hagenberg, Austria
{karl-heinz.kastner,robert.keber,petru.pau,
martin.samal}@risc.software.at

**Abstract.** ITS Austria West is a long-term project, funded by the Austrian government, to create a platform for providing real-time traffic data and prognoses. The calculation of the traffic situation is based on the open source package SUMO (Simulation of Urban MObility). One innovation in this project is the *scenario builder*, a module which maintains the origin/destination matrix and aggregates data from various sources, like traffic counters and floating car data. The simulation model is continuously calibrated in order to provide an accurate view of the traffic situation in the whole street network. The calculated level-of-service information is visualized and exported to other intelligent transport systems. Due to the complexity of the model (streets, vehicles and real-time data), the simulation's performance is unsatisfactory. A possible improvement is the parallelization of SUMO.

**Keywords:** Traffic simulation · Traffic condition · Parallel computing

## 1 Introduction

Predictably, the future Intelligent Transport Systems (ITS) will make a significant contribution to secure our long-term mobility. Challenges facing such systems include intelligent handling of the increasing traffic by use of efficient multimodal transport, as well as the need to a balanced use of existing transport infrastructure. In this respect, the availability of reliable real-time traffic information to all stakeholders (institutions, companies and individuals) is necessary.

The project ITS Austria West aims at providing a traffic data platform which generates accurate information regarding the current traffic situation, based on a (limited) number of traffic data sources and on historical information regarding vehicle trips on Upper Austrian roads. For the computation of current status of each road, as well as for short-term prognoses, the traffic simulation package SUMO is used.

In this paper we describe the concepts of ITS Austria West and focus on the integration of SUMO, and its results, into the real-time traffic data platform.

Section 2 contains an overview of the ITS Austria West project, its architecture and short descriptions of the main components. In Sect. 3 we describe the integration of SUMO package within ITS Austria West and give some technical details about our approach to a parallel SUMO. Section 4 contains some ideas about consuming the results – using the traffic information provided by SUMO to define level-of-service

© Springer-Verlag Berlin Heidelberg 2014
M. Behrisch et al. (Eds.): SUMO 2013, LNCS 8594, pp. 146–159, 2014.
DOI: 10.1007/978-3-662-45079-6_11

values that can be used to describe synthetically the current traffic status. We end with some conclusions and future extensions.

## 2   ITS Austria West

The main goal of the project ITS Austria West is to continuously provide real-time snapshots of the traffic situation in Upper Austria and Salzburg to the VAO service (Verkehrsauskunft Österreich – Austrian Traffic Information System, [5]). Project partners are the state Upper Austria, the state Salzburg, RISC Software GmbH, Salzburg Research and Logistikum Steyr. The project is funded by the Austrian KLIEN fond ("Klima- und Energiefond") and by the Upper Austrian government. It started in June 2011 and ends in September 2014.

The underlying street network is based on data provided by GIP [2] ("Graphen-integrationsplattform"), a database which comprises all Austrian highways, interstate and municipal roads, as well as local, low-ranked streets. The GIP database was created in the frame of a previous project conducted by all nine states of Austria. This database is intended as a starting point for many current and future applications.

In order to create a real-time snapshot for the state of Upper Austria, up-to-date traffic data is crucial. Various data sources are utilized: stationary vehicle counters, as well as floating car data (FCD).

### 2.1   ITS Austria West: Architecture

Conceptually, the software realizing the tasks of ITS Austria West consists of:

– components handling the *sensor data*;
– components for *visualizing* or *publishing results*;
– a *simulation environment*;
– a module in charge with *generating* and *running scenarios*, and
– a *management component*.

Figure 1 gives an overview of the system architecture, whose main components are explained in the following paragraphs.

The controlling part of the ITS West Austria Management System is the *management console*, where all processes are created, parameterized and controlled.

The *scenario builder*, triggered by the console, is responsible for the periodic creation of new scenarios, which serve as basis for the simulation of the traffic for the next time interval. This complex component works with a model of the Upper Austrian road network, and uses the real-time sensor data, together with the output of running simulations, to generate periodically snapshots of the traffic status.

Computed values of the traffic status (summarized as *level of services* – LoS, see [3]) are made available in various ways. An important outlet is a set of WMS layers (*web map service*, see [4]), published and made available via a website: The roads with delays or traffic jams are marked with standardized colors, as well as the portions with road works or roadblocks.

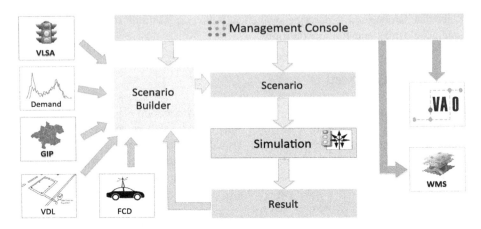

**Fig. 1.** ITS Austria west management system: system architecture.

Since not all roads are covered by sensors, some way to extrapolate the known, real-time traffic values to the uncovered streets has to be realized. We use traffic simulation applications to estimate traffic values on *all* roads of the street network. The *simulation environment* makes it possible to start simulations (SUMO, for the moment, but other systems are under consideration as well), to communicate with them, and to extract their results.

The *sensor data module* receives information from different types of sensors:

1. *Vehicle detection loops* (VDL) are stationary detectors which count the number of vehicles and their velocity. About 80 *vehicle detection cells*, owned by the Upper Austrian government, are installed on the main streets. *Road maintenance data*, also owned by the Upper Austrian government, are used to detect streets with road-blocks. Last but not least, the Austrian highway agency ASFINAG streams up-to-date information for the 2.178 km Austrian highways.

2. *Floating car data* is provided by the Austrian emergency rescue service "Samar-iterbund" (only from vehicles that are not in action), some taxi fleets and a worldwide GPS tracking company.

The *VLSA configuration* contains locations of the traffic lights and the logic behind their functioning. Based on the VLSA, the *crossroads with traffic lights* are identified and integrated in the internal street network.

The *demand model*, i.e. the origin/destination matrix, is provided by the Upper Austrian authorities and adapted using historical traffic data on Upper Austrian roads. From the raw data collected from stationary sensors, time-variation curves with the traffic values are computed and, based on these curves, the routes from the original demand model are temporally distributed during one day. These routes serve as input for the simulation tools.

# 3   Traffic Simulation

In order to fill up gaps in the network coverage with sensors, traffic simulation applications offer an attractive alternative. Such applications, developed since the 1950s, can be classified in microscopic, mesoscopic and macroscopic.

In a microscopic model every vehicle is simulated. Such a model contains a detailed street graph, with traffic lights and turn lanes, and a demand model – an origin/destination matrix.

Mesoscopic models describe the traffic entities (roads and vehicles) at an equal level of detail, but their behavior and interactions are described at a lower level of detail.

In macroscopic models all parts are simulated in a lower detail. Traffic flow values are computed and maintained, rather than individual vehicles.

Main commercial providers of traffic simulation applications are PTV (with VISUM), Aimsun, Caliper and UAF, but for development purposes, the free, open-source simulation tool SUMO is among the most interesting.

The computation power of nowadays computers makes it possible to use microscopic traffic simulation applications even for large-scale models, or real-life models. These tools should provide the maximum level of accuracy in modelling and predicting the values of traffic for whole geographic areas, during prolonged periods of time.

They come, however, with some challenges:

1. Modelling the road network: Problems arise from inexactitudes in data, and from the tradeoff between the efficiency requirements (i.e., keeping the number of streets as small as possible) and accuracy requirements (i.e., how well the road network model represents the real street network).
2. Modelling the routes: The demand model provided by authorities becomes quickly obsolete, due to the highly dynamical social and economic conditions in the modelled region.
3. Inherent complexity of the simulation: Microscopic traffic simulation applications handle every action of every vehicle, which might lead to millions of operations per second.

## 3.1   Using SUMO for ITS Austria West

SUMO is an open source, microscopic simulation package developed by the German Aerospace Center (DLR) in 2001. It is not only a traffic simulation, but rather a suite of applications which help prepare and perform the simulation of traffic [1].

In order to be able to employ SUMO in ITS Austria West, a model of the road network and a model of the trips (with the full definition of the roads for each trip) must be available.

The *road network* is generated periodically from the latest version of the GIP database. Additional information comes from the Upper Austrian traffic light system and from the stationary vehicle sensors. With this input, a SUMO network is generated, in which the roads, intersections, turning relations, traffic lights and vehicle induction loops are modeled.

The set of *daily routes* is computed in a complex process in which the trips contained in the origin-destination matrix are distributed along the daily time variation curves.

## 3.2 Simulation Run

In order to offer a realistic and useful view of the traffic status, periodical snapshots are sufficient. Every few minutes traffic data collected from sensors or provided by a simulation must be integrated into such a snapshot.

There are two ways in which a traffic simulation tool can be used:

1. The simulation application is started at the beginning of a time interval; it runs for a time (5 min simulation time), and then exits. The output is collected and interpreted. Figure 2 contains a graphical representation of this process.
2. The simulation application runs continuously. At the beginning of a time interval, the next 5 min are simulated. When the simulation of this interval is completed, the results are collected and, if necessary, the model is adjusted (calibrated) on-the-fly. (A graphical depiction of this process can be seen in Fig. 3)

Regardless in which way the simulation is used, calibrations need to be performed periodically. They might comprise vehicle re-routing, insertion of new vehicles or removal of some vehicles already in the network. Also, the speed on some roads might need to be changed, due to events which occurred in the reality.

It turned out that simply loading the whole model in SUMO takes prohibitively long (about one minute or more). In the first, start-and-exit model, considerable time is used up by initialization; even if the simulation runs exceedingly fast, too little time remains for the tasks that need to be executed after the simulation has finished

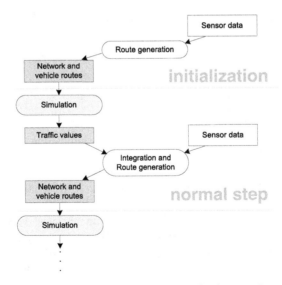

**Fig. 2.** Running more instances of the simulation application, one in each time interval.

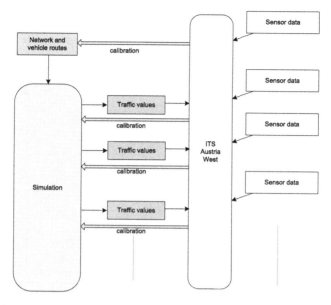

**Fig. 3.** Running one instance of the simulation application, with periodic calibration and output.

(interpretation of results, aggregation of real-time data, generation of data for WMS layers, preparation of data for the next simulation interval).

We decided to implement the second, always-running model.

**Managing a Running SUMO Simulation.** From the management console, an instance of the simulation application is started and communication mechanisms are set in place.

We use TraCI (**Tra**ffic **C**ontrol **I**nterface) API to send orders to SUMO. For extracting results, with the *status* of every vehicle currently running, and with the statistics collected by vehicle induction loops, we use the socket-based dumping mechanisms implemented in SUMO.

Figure 4 shows the activities taking place in the simulation and in ITS Austria West during a time interval.

At the beginning of the interval, calibration orders are sent to SUMO via TraCI. They are immediately followed by a "Simulate To" order, which commands SUMO to perform a simulation up to the end of the current interval, in simulation time.

SUMO integrates the changes contained in the calibration orders (adding new vehicles, removing or re-routing existing vehicle) and immediately starts to simulate the traffic. When the end of the currently simulated interval is reached, SUMO puts the traffic values on the dump socket and waits until next "SimulateTo" is received.

Ideally, SUMO finishes the simulation *before* the end of the current interval in real time. If this is the case, the simulation management component is able to do its work; the synchronisation of the simulation with the reality is possible.

The SUMO output is collected and interpreted by the simulation management component of ITS Austria West. If it disagrees with the latest real-time data received from sensors, new calibration orders are generated accordingly.

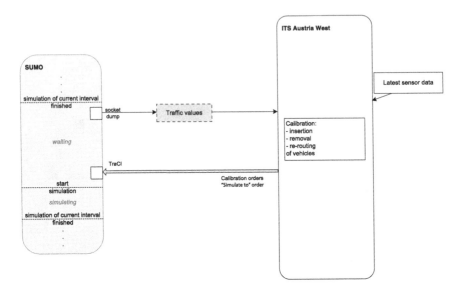

**Fig. 4.** Communication between SUMO and ITS Austria West.

More importantly, however, the output of SUMO can be used for the generation of the traffic snapshots issued by ITS Austria West: For streets not monitored by vehicle counters, or not described by floating car data – streets where the traffic situation is otherwise unknown – we can use traffic values obtained from the simulation. The integration of simulation data into the traffic snapshots is optional and can be turned on or off in the management console.

We described above the use of SUMO in a *real-time scenario*. It should be mentioned, however, that ITS Austria West allows working with a simulation tool in *calibration mode* as well, where synchronisation with the real time is not necessary and historical traffic data, for each currently simulated time interval, are used instead of the latest traffic data. The purpose of running a simulation in calibration mode is to obtain a *calibrated demand model*. Expectedly, the traffic situation obtained by running simulations with a calibrated demand model approximates better the situation on the roads.

### 3.3 Parallelism

In order to work in a real environment, the simulation must perform considerably faster than real-time. Several tests have shown that the rush hours, in Upper Austria, cannot be in fact simulated by SUMO faster than real-time.

The most immediate way to speed things up is the parallelization of the software. To achieve this goal, the existing SUMO single-threaded calculation model need to be reengineered and converted into a multi-threaded model, where the new positions of the cars are calculated in parallel.

We describe in the following our experiments for parallel SUMO and conclude with a few results. It will become apparent that a profound reengineering is necessary in order to obtain an efficient version of parallel SUMO.

All technical details refer to SUMO version 0.17. In newer versions, names of some functions mentioned here may have been changed.

For the simulation of the traffic in a working day, routes were generated according to statistical data received from official, governmental institutions. In Upper Austria only, the total number of vehicles driving daily exceeds one million. As expected, the highest density of vehicles occurs during the rush hours – 5 to 9, and 15 to 19 – when more than 100 thousand vehicles are simultaneously on the roads.

When given as input to Sumo, these routes lead to an unsatisfactory simulation speed of the traffic, starting from 6:00am simulated time. The efficiency of Sumo decreases steadily, reaching levels where the simulated time runs slower than the real time.

This fact challenged us to look for ways to parallelize the heavy work load. A quick profiling showed the functions in which Sumo spends most of the time, during an internal simulation step (see Fig. 5). Further investigations revealed that the function `MSTLLogicControl::setTrafficLightSignals` can be easily parallelized, but for the other two relevant functions, `MSEdgeControl::moveFirst` and `MSEdgeControl::moveCritical`, the parallelization is not trivial. Also, when the number of routes starting in a small time interval is extremely high, the program spends a significant amount of time in the function `MSInsertionControl::emitVehicles` and therefore it also needs to be considered for parallelization.

Our first attempt at parallelization involved OpenMP and was a brute-force approach. Steps in highest-level "`for`"-loops were executed in parallel; critical sections were defined to forbid concurrent access to data structures, if these data structures were being modified from at least one thread. This approach, its shortcomings and some results will be described in the next section.

All subsequent discussions refer to adapting and compiling SUMO within Microsoft Visual Studio 10, on Windows 7 platforms.

**Using OpenMP in a Minimally-Invasive Parallelization.** In our first approach, we used OpenMP directives to define code blocks executed in parallel. Where concurrent access, especially in writing, was not desired, we defined critical sections.

The OpenMP standard provided by the C++ compiler in Visual Studio 10 does not allow parallelization of "`for`"-loops where the loop variable is an STL iterator. Since the main "`for`"-loops in the three functions mentioned above are driven by iterators over STL containers, some artificial constructs are needed in order to use the OpenMP "`for`" directive.

In fact, starting a parallel thread for each step of those for loops is not computationally efficient, due to the considerable overhead involved. We decided to split the affected STL containers beforehand; each part is then processed in its own thread.

This simple strategy is clearly effective when the STL containers do not change after initialization – like the elements processed in function `MSTLLogicControl::setTrafficLightSignals`. Here, a number of iterator domains are defined on the container with traffic light logics, as soon as the initialization of this container ends. Using OpenMP "`for`" directive, in `MSTLLogicControl::setTrafficLightSignals`, each iterator domain is processed in a separate thread, in which a local iterator runs over the current domain.

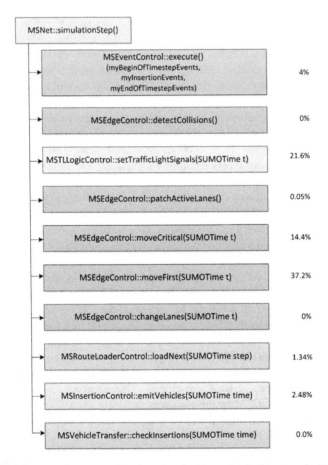

MSNet::simulationStep()

MSEventControl::execute()
(myBeginOfTimestepEvents,
myInsertionEvents,
myEndOfTimestepEvents)                    4%

MSEdgeControl::detectCollisions()          0%

MSTLLogicControl::setTrafficLightSignals(SUMOTime t)    21.6%

MSEdgeControl::patchActiveLanes()          0.05%

MSEdgeControl::moveCritical(SUMOTime t)    14.4%

MSEdgeControl::moveFirst(SUMOTime t)       37.2%

MSEdgeControl::changeLanes(SUMOTime t)     0%

MSRouteLoaderControl::loadNext(SUMOTime step)    1.34%

MSInsertionControl::emitVehicles(SUMOTime time)    2.48%

MSVehicleTransfer::checkInsertions(SUMOTime time)    0.0%

**Fig. 5.** The most important functions invoked in a simulation step, in SUMO.

The objects processed in the other two functions, MSEdgeControl:: move-First and MSEdgeControl::moveCritical, are *active lanes*, i.e., lanes which contain vehicles. Active lanes can be removed from this container in both functions; lanes becoming active are added to the container in MSEdgeControl:: move-First. A splitting strategy similar to that described above would need a re-computation of the iterator domains at the end of each of these two functions, and would involve essentially a sequential traversal of the container.

We use an alternative strategy, namely an array of STL containers. Each element of this array is processed in a separate thread, started by an OpenMP "for" directive, in both functions MSEdgeControl::moveFirst and MSEdgeControl:: moveCritical. Lanes which were not active, but in the current step contain vehicles, are added after the parallel section of MSEdgeControl:: moveCritical has finished; these new lanes are evenly distributed among the containers in the array.

Some internal data structures in classes MSVehicle, MSLane and MSLink are accessed and modified from functions that may be running, at the same time, in different threads. Since STL containers are not multithreaded-safe, mechanisms must be provided to avoid multiple access. The first idea was to use again OpenMP directives, namely to define *critical sections*.

With an OpenMP "`critical`" directive, blocks of code are marked with a name that identifies a critical section. If a thread gets hold of a marked block, any other thread attempting to run a block marked with the same name must wait until the running block is freed.

We defined a set of critical sections to restrict the access to internal data structures for vehicles, lanes and links.

This approach has two important shortcomings:

1. The critical sections restrict access to portions of code, rather than to shared data. As a consequence, processing the vehicles on a street in Berlin, for example, must wait until the same kind of processing finishes the vehicles on a street in Leipzig, although they can – and should – be processed in parallel without restrictions. In other words, the threads must wait for one another although there may be no reason to do that.
2. In every processing step (once every second simulation time) a number of threads are generated – once in `MSEdgeControl::moveFirst` and once in `MSEdgeControl::moveCritical` – and closed. While small, the involved overhead is not negligible.

The alternative to critical sections is to define *locks* (by means of, e.g., mutexes) as members of each instance of `MSVehicle`, `MSLane` and `MSLink`. Whenever a critical structure is being accessed, the lock shall be activated; at the end of the processing, the lock shall be released.

The conceivable overhead for this alternative is not negligible, both in memory consumption and computation effort. Our first experiments revealed that, indeed, parallelization with locking objects defined for each element (lane, link, and vehicle) is even slower than the sequential SUMO, and the memory consumption increases drastically.

**OpenMP Parallelization: Results.** In our tests we used a version of the modified SUMO console application (version 0.16) adapted for 2, 4 and 8 threads: Two, four and respectively eight iterator domains were defined for the traffic lights, arrays of containers with similar lengths for the active lanes. We ran this version on a computer with four cores with hyperthreading at 3.4 GHz, and 8 Gb RAM.

For a moderately large network and set of vehicles, the best results were obtained with the 4-thread parallel version. It finished the simulation in about 65 % of the time needed by the sequential version. This network was randomly generated, with 150000 edges. The 20 000 routes were also randomly generated; the maximum number of vehicles simultaneously on the roads was around 3500.

For a large network (whole Upper Austria), after the first 25 000 s, the 4-thread parallel version took only 57 % from the time needed by the sequential version. The maximum number of vehicles simultaneously on the roads was around 80 000; more than 263 000 vehicles have been generated.

Parallel versions with two and eight threads proved to be less efficient. In the 2-thread version, the overhead did not pay off: the gain in efficiency, for the parallelized part, was too small. In the 8-thread version, the number of threads competing to execute critical sections led to prohibitively long waiting times.

Exact results, with the time spent by SUMO in each relevant function, are shown in Table 1.

**Alternative Approaches to Parallelization.** The brute-force parallelization is inherently limited, if no additional information about the network and/or vehicle routes is employed. Generating a number of threads in each simulation steps, threads that afterwards compete to gain access to shared data structures, cannot lead to efficient, scalable parallel versions of SUMO.

A more elaborate approach at parallelization should start by splitting the underlying data structures using some topological criteria. From the original sets of roads, junctions, traffic lights, etc., *sub-networks* should be defined. The number of connections between different sub-networks should be as small as possible.

The simulation should proceed on each sub-network in parallel, so that each thread runs its own simulation loop. Synchronization points should be defined, in order to keep fast threads from running ahead. Also, vehicles that jump over sub-network boundaries should be processed in a sequential manner: It must be ensured that no multiple accesses to the data structures affected in this processing step occur.

It is clear to us that this approach requires a significant re-engineering of SUMO, starting with a design oriented towards parallelism. While the foreseeable effort is considerable, we are confident that a fully parallel, scalable version would provide the efficiency needed to simulate large-scale, real-life traffic situations.

## 4    Project Outcomes

Based on the information available during a simulation run, the *level-of-service* (LoS) should be calculated. The term "level-of-service" has been defined differently over the time. The origin of this definition comes from the transportation planning in the U.S., where this notion was defined for the service quality of road infrastructure. The traditional level-of-service is available in 6 categories, from A (for free ride) to F (for gridlock). The details are set out in the Highway Capacity Manual [3]. In Europe usually only the traffic-light colours are used (green: free travel, orange: slow-moving traffic and red: traffic jam). Additionally, the colour Black can represent gridlocks.

In our case, the level-of-service is extracted from traffic information associated to relevant edges: To every edge of the road network with a computed density of traffic (either from real-time data or from SUMO), a level-of-service is assigned.

The image in Fig. 6 shows the LoS information generated from a SUMO instance, without real-time data, using MapWindow (an open-source GIS) to display the relevant data.

Eventually, a public web site shall exist where the information shall be provided by means of *web map service* (WMS) layers, one for each LoS degree. A mobile app, developed for a large range of mobile devices, will integrate the WMS and background (e.g. Google Maps, OpenStreetMaps) layers. Figure 7 offers a preview of the web site. The road works and roadblocks are also visible.

**Table 1.** Time spent by SUMO in the most relevant function, in a processing step.

| | Random network (150 000 edges 20 000 route) | Upper Austria (180 000 edges, 1 200 000 routes) |
|---|---|---|
| **Sequential** | After 13600 steps and 182.661 seconds: | After 25000 steps and 1128.699 seconds: |
| | Timestep Events: 9.012 seconds | Timestep Events: 13.493 seconds |
| | setTrafficLightSignals: 35.213 seconds | setTrafficLightSignals: 62.747 seconds |
| | patchActiveLanes: 0.041 seconds | patchActiveLanes: 0.128 seconds |
| | moveCritical: 33.23 seconds | moveCritical: 348.401 seconds |
| | moveFirst: 39.986 seconds | moveFirst: 426.741 seconds |
| | changeLanes: 0.003 seconds | changeLanes: 95.919 seconds |
| | loadNext: 2.005 seconds | loadNext: 17.874 seconds |
| | emitVehicles: 2.148 seconds | emitVehicles: 34.950 seconds |
| | checkInsertion: 0.002 seconds | checkInsertion: 20.176 seconds |
| **Parallel (2 threads)** | After 13500 steps and 152 seconds: | After 25000 steps and 820.784 seconds: |
| | Timestep Events: 10.169 seconds | Timestep Events: 14.775 seconds |
| | setTrafficLightSignals: 29.004 seconds | setTrafficLightSignals: 40.176 seconds |
| | patchActiveLanes: 0.04 seconds | patchActiveLanes: 0.126 seconds |
| | moveCritical: 24.438 seconds | moveCritical: 231.840 seconds |
| | moveFirst: 30.979 seconds | moveFirst: 257.587 seconds |
| | changeLanes: 0.009 seconds | changeLanes: 102.652 seconds |
| | loadNext: 2.103 seconds | loadNext: 18.569 seconds |
| | emitVehicles: 2.322 seconds | emitVehicles: 34.468 seconds |
| | checkInsertion: 0.002 seconds | checkInsertion: 22.728 seconds |
| **Parallel (4 threads)** | After 13500 steps and 119.1 seconds: | After 25000 steps and 649.733 seconds: |
| | Timestep Events: 9.085 seconds | Timestep Events: 13.687 seconds |
| | setTrafficLightSignals: 21.673 seconds | setTrafficLightSignals: 25.024 seconds |
| | patchActiveLanes: 0.036 seconds | patchActiveLanes: 0.113 seconds |
| | moveCritical: 15.3 seconds | moveCritical: 174.939 seconds |
| | moveFirst: 18.19 seconds | moveFirst: 173.349 seconds |
| | changeLanes: 0.009 seconds | changeLanes: 103.212 seconds |
| | loadNext: 2.01 seconds | loadNext: 18.653 seconds |
| | emitVehicles: 2.249 seconds | emitVehicles: 34.901 seconds |
| | checkInsertion: 0.001 seconds | checkInsertion: 23.766 seconds |
| **Parallel (8 threads)** | After 13600 steps and 133.35 seconds: | After 25000 steps and 798.479 seconds: |
| | Timestep Events: 9.87 seconds | Timestep Events: 15.934 seconds |
| | setTrafficLightSignals: 26.465 seconds | setTrafficLightSignals: 33.021 seconds |
| | patchActiveLanes: 0.034 seconds | patchActiveLanes: 0.129 seconds |
| | moveCritical: 19.78 seconds | moveCritical: 209.453 seconds |
| | moveFirst: 26.96 seconds | moveFirst: 236.049 seconds |
| | changeLanes: 0.011 seconds | changeLanes: 144.329 seconds |
| | loadNext: 2.391 seconds | loadNext: 23.945 seconds |
| | emitVehicles: 2.951 seconds | emitVehicles: 43.803 seconds |
| | checkInsertion: 0.006 seconds | checkInsertion: 30.203 seconds |

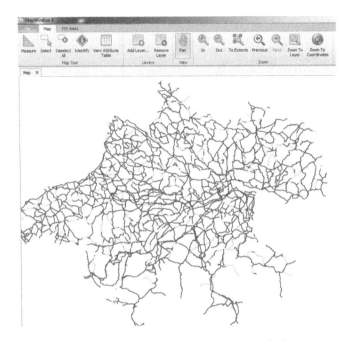

**Fig. 6.** LoS mapping in an open-source GIS.

**Fig. 7.** Preview of the web page with WMS layers offering the LoS for Upper Austrian roads. The background is obtained from OpenStreetMaps.

# 5  Conclusions and Future Work

In this paper we described a system that employs SUMO as a core simulation system for computing short-term traffic data starting from a given traffic situations and a dynamically adjusted demand model. The traffic status at the end of the simulation is adjusted with real-time data coming from networks of sensors and stands as basis for the next short-term simulation.

For the street network of Upper Austria, and for real-life scenarios, the efficiency of SUMO decreased below real-time. We described in Sect. 3.3 our attempt at parallelizing SUMO. While imperfect and, in fact, not efficient enough, our parallel-SUMO prototype showed that the multithreaded approach yields significant speed improvements.

We described how SUMO is currently used in ITS Austria West, synchronized with the real time; we intend to use SUMO for a *short-term prognosis*, in which the next 30 min, or more, are simulated. This prognosis will be used to study the effect of various changes in the street network, coming from e.g. accidents, road works, or different speed limits.

To improve the quality of the prognosis, the existing sensor network will be further expanded, which should lead to a faster recognition of traffic disruptions. The generated real-time traffic condition is considered as a basis for a dynamic traffic information system and adaptive traffic control systems.

# References

1. Behrisch, M., Bieker, L., Erdmann, J., Krajzewicz, D.: SUMO - simulation of Urban MObility: an overview. In: SIMUL 2011, Barcelona, Spain, pp. 63–68 (2011)
2. http://www.gip.gv.at. 10 Jan 2013
3. Highway Capacity Manual, Transportation Research Board, National Research Council, 3rd edn., 5 (1985) (updated 1994)
4. http://www.opengeospatial.org/standards/wms
5. http://www.gip.gv.at/VAO-en.html

# SUMO in Scientific Literature, 2002–2012

Daniel Krajzewicz[✉]

German Aerospace Center, Institute of Transportation Systems,
Berlin, Germany
daniel.krajzewicz@dlr.de

**Abstract.** SUMO is an open source microscopic road traffic simulation developed at the German Aerospace Center since the year 2000. The major audience is the traffic research community. This article tries to answer whether SUMO got accepted, who uses it, and for which purposes. The investigation is performed based on a collection of scientific publications that name SUMO. The documents contained in this collection were bibliographically annotated and classified using three different classification schemes. The investigation reveals an increasing usage of SUMO by a growing, international community. It shows that SUMO is mainly used in the scope of research on vehicular communications.

**Keywords:** Simulation system · Applications · Bibliography · Faceted classification

## 1 Introduction

"Simulation of Urban Mobility" (SUMO, [1, 2]) is an open source road traffic simulation package that is continuously developed since the year 2000. It simulates how individually described and processed vehicles move along streets of a given road network model, regarding maximum velocities, road use restrictions and right-of-way rules at passed intersections. SUMO supports a large set of models for the vehicles' longitudinal behavior – so-called car-following models – as well as for lane changing. It allows to model different vehicle types that differ in length, maximum velocity, acceleration and deceleration possibilities, pollutant emission behavior, etc. Modelling public transport is supported as well. Besides vehicles and the road network, the simulation can handle additional infrastructure facilities, such as traffic lights that support different standard actuation algorithms, bus stops, or simulated detectors of different kind.

The simulation itself is accompanied by several further applications that allow importing and generating road networks for the simulator, as well as tools for generating the vehicles to simulate and/or computing their routes based on different methods and paradigms. The simulation package includes a simulation application with a graphical interface. The other tools contained in the package have to be started and configured via the command line. SUMO is mainly developed at the Institute of Transportation Systems at the German Aerospace Center and is licensed under the GPL. The motivation for making the software available under an open license was to support the traffic research community with a common test bed for models and solutions under development. The first public version was released in 2002.

M. Behrisch et al. (Eds.): SUMO 2013, LNCS 8594, pp. 160–174, 2014.
DOI: 10.1007/978-3-662-45079-6_12

As indicated by this short summary, a feature-rich application system has been developed over a long time span with frequent publicly available updates. But, is SUMO a success story? Has it found its acceptance and what is it used for? Who uses it? These questions are tried to be answered in the following by evaluating scientific literature that cites SUMO. The investigations presented here are based upon the work reported in [3], extending it by further evaluations and explanations.

Section 2 outlines the used methodology of this investigation. Section 3 presents the documents collection, describing how it was generated and discussing its coverage and quality. The applied faceted classification is presented in Sect. 4. The results of evaluating the annotated collection are given in Sect. 5. This report ends with a summary.

## 2  Methodology

Often, the popularity of a software package is measured using its download numbers. This indicator has some drawbacks, mainly because it is not known whether a human being or a software robot downloaded the software and for which purpose. This at least counts for unrestricted downloads as used for SUMO deployment. Other systems that ask the downloader to register before downloading could have been used but were dismissed for SUMO. Shortly after being released for the first time, SUMO could have been found on several open source download portals, additionally blurring the available download statistics.

Of course, other sources of information exist. Most of the communication between SUMO users and developers takes place via mailing lists. But it is known from observation that some users were able to use SUMO in their research without ever occurring on the mailing list. One could as well use usual web page popularity measurement techniques, such as access counters, URL evaluation, Google rank etc. In fact, none of these methods were applied to SUMO's web presence. Further web-based tools that could be evaluated (wiki, bug tracker, blog) were introduced incrementally over SUMO's development time. Therefore, they do not cover the first years of SUMO's availability.

But when reminding what SUMO was designed for – to support the traffic research community with a common test bed for models and solutions – a further source of information gets available, namely scientific reports ("publications"). The scientific community usually publishes new results (albeit usually only reporting about successful research) as printable documents – either monographs or parts of a collection, such as a journal or the proceedings of a conference. The copyright usually allows to include these documents on own web pages where "own" usually denotes the organization the authors belong to. Such publicly available documents are usually given as PDF files for download. Due to being available publicly and because the full text can usually be extracted from such documents, they can be found using web search engines. The major advantage of using scientific reports is the possibility to extract a large set of different information, including the topic of the work, the authors, the time of being published, to name a few. This goes far beyond pure counting of a certain event like a download.

One could be attempted to assign the work presented here to a scientific methodology. In principle, two methodologies are used. The first is "citation analysis", here based on bibliographic references generated for the used documents' collection. One should note that all types of naming SUMO in scientific literature are used instead of tracking citations of one or a set of documents, The second methodology applied in this research is a "biographical classification" using a faceted classification.

# 3    The Documents Collection

The evaluation of scientific literature on SUMO presented herein is based on a set of documents, named "the collection" in the following. Besides the documents themselves, the evaluation relies on the bibliographic references that represent the collection's documents. The following sub-sections present and discuss the collection, starting with a description about how it was generated. Whether the collection includes all documents that name SUMO or at least is a statistically valid sample of this set is discussed afterwards. The overview of the collection closes with a discussion of the correctness of the bibliographic references.

## 3.1    Building the Collection

Most of the documents were obtained by searching the web using Google [4] and other web search engines. The search was performed between the years 2002 and 2012 repeatedly, albeit spontaneously and not following any fixed frequency or any certain event. Usually, combinations of terms such as "SUMO", "traffic simulation", or "Simulation of Urban Mobility" were used. Often, the term "Krajzewicz" was added, as none of the previously named search terms references to the object of research only. In all cases, the results retrieved from search engines had to be filtered. Mainly, because the results always contain links to web resources that do not deal with the SUMO traffic simulation at all. But additionally many links point to documentation pages, download portals, or other projects that cite or use SUMO and which are of no value for the investigation presented here.

For the so collected documents, the bibliographic information was obtained. Initially, this was done by searching the web for respectively given references to the publication and using those. To obtain the references of later (starting in 2011) gathered documents, Google Scholar [5] was used as well. In these cases, the title of the publication was used as the search term[1] in Google Scholar. From the results, the entry with the same title and the same authors as the original document was chosen. No ambiguities were observed during this process. In both cases, the references were stored in a BibTeX-database [6, 7].

Starting in 2011, additional Google Scholar "alerts" [8] have been used to get informed about new publications that cite SUMO. When established, a Google Scholar alert sends mails to its owner as soon as Google Scholar receives a new document

---

[1] Not as "exact search".

containing certain key words. Two alerts were set up, one tracking the search terms "'traffic simulation' SUMO", and one tracking the term "Krajewicz". The links sent by Google Scholar often point to digital library portals, such as Springer Link [9], IEEE Xplore [10], ScienceDirect [11], or ACM Digital Library [12]. Usually, these portals do not only allow to download the publication itself but also its bibliographic information. In such cases, the bibliographic information was directly stored as a BibTeX-entry in a BibTeX-database. In cases where Google Scholar pointed directly to a PDF (the document itself), the bibliographic information was determined as outlined before for the documents collected using web search engines.

After presenting [3], the database was tried to be enriched by further documents. The major source were Google Scholar alerts defined as described above. Additional searches via web engines were performed as well. In sum, 45 documents were obtained that were not yet in the collection. Almost all of these documents are from 2012, only one from the year 2010. This yields in an imbalanced view, at least regarding the development of the publication number.

The resulting artefact is a BibTeX-formatted bibliography of papers that cite SUMO, each described by its BibTeX-entry and linked to the documents. This bibliography was cleaned. One may note that both the initially used search terms as well as the Google Scholar alert terms already force the retrieval of documents written in English language. Albeit some documents in other languages were collected, only English and German documents will be regarded in the following. Documents that were written by core developers of SUMO[2] only were excluded from the collection as well, following the wish to determine the external user's acceptance and work topics. Entries that lacked the information about the publication year or which full texts could not be obtained were also dismissed. The resulting set includes 396 publications.

## 3.2 Coverage

It can hardly be answered whether the collection is a valid sample in means of representing the set of all publications that cite SUMO correctly. The results presented in the following match the observations done while following discussions on the mailing list as well as during personal talks with SUMO users. In addition, the documents were collected using unbiased search terms, concentrating on finding information about the traffic simulation SUMO only, not a certain usage modality or topic.

One could as well ask whether all groups or persons that use SUMO, cite it and whether they should do it. SUMO is often used as a part of multi-simulator middleware architectures, such as "Veins" [13], "MOVE" [14], "VSimRTI" [15], or "iTETRIS" [16] and some publications are known where SUMO was used, but the middleware is named only. As most of such middleware solutions were developed for simulating vehicular communications, one could assume that SUMO is used within this research topic even more often than shown in Sect. 5.5. With an increasing maturity of these

---

[2] Laura Bieker, Yun-Pang Flötteröd, Michael Behrisch, Jakob Erdmann, Peter Wagner, and Daniel Krajewicz.

tools, one should as well expect that the components they use, such as SUMO, will be named less and less often.

It is not common to cite a used tool. It is a good practice nonetheless as it helps in understanding the results given in a publication by knowing the used models. As SUMO is continuously developed and changes its behavior between versions, one should name not only SUMO itself but the used version as well, in fact.

### 3.3 Bibliographic References Quality

As stated, the collection is stored as a BibTeX-database. The major attribute of a BibTeX-entry is the publication type, which determines which further attributes must be given for the according BibTeX-entry. BibTeX distinguishes between publication types such as Master thesis, PhD thesis, "inproceedings", book, or article. From BibTeX, the investigation presented here uses the attributes "title", "author", "year" as well as the publication type itself.

The BibTeX-descriptions obtained from library portals are of good quality, including all needed information and without any obvious errors. The bibliographic information from Google Scholar was often erroneous. Both, Master and Doctoral theses were often not assigned to the proper BibTeX-type. This was corrected manually as long as the correct type could be determined. Often, the publication year was not given or one could find the name of a month in the according field, instead. This was corrected manually, but the information could not be found for six documents.

Another attribute that was expected to be problematic were the author names. Dots were missing at the first name abbreviations, non-Latin characters as German "Umlaute" ("ä", "ö", or "ü") were encoded in different ways, first names were only sometimes abbreviated, and middle names not always given. This was corrected by inspecting similar names manually and putting them against other available information, such as the organization the author(s) belong to. It is assumed to be not reliable to 100 % (Table 1).

**Table 1.** Summary on the collection's bibliographic references issues

| Property | Value |
| --- | --- |
| Document number | 396 |
| BibTeX: type | Is mandatory in BibTeX, but is probably not correct for many of the documents as discussed |
| BibTeX: Year | Assumed to be correct |
| BibTeX: Journal/BibTeX: Booktitle | Assumed to be incorrect and complicated and time consuming to be corrected; neglected |
| BibTeX: Authors | Assumed to be correct to a large degree |

## 4   Faceted Classification

Each of the entries included in the collection was annotated by further attributes (predicates) that are not a part of the common BibTeX-notation. These attributes assign each document to classes that belong to three independent classification schemes. The annotation was done using JabRef [17], an open source literature management application that natively works with BibTeX-files. The following classification schemes were used: (1) SUMO's role in the reported research, (2) the topic of the publication, and (3) organization(s) the author(s) belong to. They will be discussed in the following.

(1) SUMO's role in the reported research

The first classification scheme distinguishes between the role of SUMO within the research presented in the respective publication. The following classes are used: "mentioned", "used", "extended", and "contributed". "contributed" is a subset of "extended" and is not used in the following. Each document is assigned to exactly one of the remaining three classes of this classification scheme.

The classification is assumed to be valid to a high degree. The classes were defined before classifying the documents.

(2) The topic of the publication

The second classification scheme tries to sort the publications by their main research topic. It should indeed be named as a "try", as it is semantically the most weak one of the used classification schemes. The main motivation behind this scheme was to quickly recognize in which scientific area SUMO is used or mentioned. In several cases (see Fig. 3), a document was assigned to more than one topic. Examples may be presentations of architectures for simulating vehicular communications which include descriptions of additionally developed communication models (a protocol, e.g.) as well as the evaluation of an ITS solution that uses the simulation system presented beforehand. Such a document would be assigned to the subtopics "simulation software", "routing protocols", and "applications" of the major topic "V2X".

Although several use cases for SUMO were known before classifying the collection documents, the topics were not defined a priori. Instead, new topics or sub-topics were added during the classification process when needed. After classifying all of the collection's documents, the topics were revisited for balancing them, mainly by joining less occupied topics into classes named "other" at different depths of the topics tree. It should be noted that the chosen topics, sub-topics as well as the terms used to describe them are surely dictated by the author's experience.

(3) Organization(s) the author(s) belong to

Finally, the organization or the organizations the authors of a publication belong to was determined. This was almost always possible using the information contained in the document itself. The classification is hierarchic: on the first level, the country an organization is located in is used. On the second level, the organization – mostly a university – is given. On the third level, if available, the department or the institute is used. For five publications, it was not possible to completely assign the authors to institutes. These publications were assigned to the class "unknown". Three reports, all from projects co-founded by the European Commission, are not indexed within this classification, because the organizations' their authors belong to are given as abbreviations only.

## 5   Evaluation

In the following, the collection's properties are presented. The evaluation was done using the Python [18] programming language and the matplotlib [19] module for visualization.

### 5.1   Titles

A very coarse, statistical view at the titles, shown in Fig. 1, already implies what will be discussed in Sect. 5.5 about research topics of the collection: the dominance of research on vehicular communications.

**Fig. 1.** Frequency of words within the collection's titles, generated with Wordle™.

For ignoring the inflexion of words their stem was determined using Porter stemming [20, 21]. Word stems obtained from the Porter algorithm are usually pruned so much that no real English word is obtained. Therefore, instead of the stem itself, the shortest complete word that was found within the titles was used. To obtain Fig. 1, the resulting list of occurrences per word was visualized using Wordle™ [22]. For stemming, the Python Porter stemming implementation from Vivake Gupta and Danny Yoo was used [23].

### 5.2   Development Over Time

Figure 2 shows the development of the annual publication number over time, distinguishing the publications' BibTeX-types. The overall development shows a fair increase over the years, albeit with some dents. The publication types were used even though they were reported to be erroneous to show the remarkable amount of theses.

As discussed, the large amount of publications from 2012 is assumed to be an artefact resulting from additionally incorporating Google Scholar since 2011. It is assumed that more references are stored in Google Scholar, but only recent publications are returned.

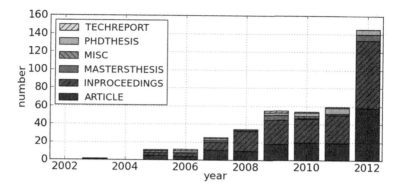

**Fig. 2.** The development of publications over the years, divided by publication type.

## 5.3    Authors and Authorship

The publications are authored by 936 persons in sum; the development is shown in Fig. 3. In this Figure, "all" denotes the set of all authors that have co-authored a document in a given year. "new" is a subset of "all" that contains authors who have not (co-)authored an earlier publication. "single" is a subset of "new", which contains authors who have contributed to one publication within the collection only.

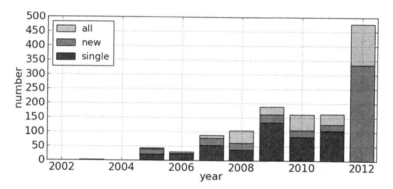

**Fig. 3.** The development of authors over the years, classified by the continuity of their publications from the collection.

Albeit the number of "all" authors is growing, the majority of the authors has participated in one publication only. This could be interpreted as a minor acceptance, but is rather supposed to have its reasons in a high number of co-authors. Often, a document describes a larger project and only few of the documents' authors have used SUMO by themselves.

## 5.4    SUMO's Role

The manual classification of documents by the role of SUMO within the reported research is maybe the best indicator for SUMO's acceptance in the scientific community. As shown in Fig. 4, not only the number of documents that report about using SUMO is increasing over time, but also the percentage of such documents. In parallel, the percentage of documents where SUMO was mentioned is decreasing even though their absolute number is relatively constant.

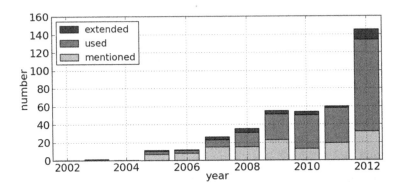

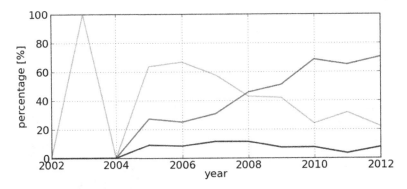

**Fig. 4.** Role of SUMO within the evaluated publications. Top: absolute numbers, bottom: percentage, both along the years.

Also remarkable is the almost constant percentage of documents where extensions to SUMO are reported. In 2008, the application control interface "TraCI" was introduced which allows an on-line interaction with the simulation. As SUMO can be controlled by an external application via TraCI, one could assume a reduction of extensions to SUMO since that time. But such a reduction can neither be observed in the absolute numbers nor within the percentages.

## 5.5    Research Topics

As described in Sect. 4, a document may be assigned to more than one research topics. Figure 5 shows the co-occurrence of topics. Topics which do not occur in combination with other topics are not shown, herein.

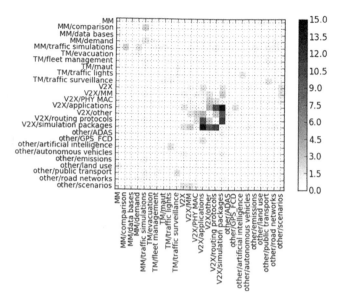

**Fig. 5.** Co-occurrences of topics within the collection. Topics with no co-occurrence are not shown. The abbreviations are: MM: mobility models, TM: traffic managements.

The development of the topics addressed within the collection over time is shown in Fig. 6. Clearly evident is the domination of documents which describe work on "V2X". In sum, about 70 % of the documents from the collection were classified into this topic. About 12 % present work on "mobility models". "traffic management" was addressed by about 10 % of the publications and "other" is discussed in about 8 %.

The dominance of V2X research within the SUMO user community was already observed and reported in [1] and the evaluation of the topics proves it. It may be also noted, that, vice versa, SUMO is the most often used traffic simulation tool in V2X research, as reported in [24]. The reasons can only be guessed. The first documents targeting this topic occur in the year 2005. One of those, "MOVE: A MObility model generator for VEhicular network" by Feliz Kristianto Karnadi, Zhi Hai Mo, and Kun-Chan Lan [25], may be the reason for SUMO's prominence in this research field. [25] presents "MOVE", a complete system for generating vehicular traces that can be used in the ns-2 simulator, which was state-of-the-art for communication simulation at that time. Screenshots of different scenarios show the system's variability in use. Whether [25] was the seed to SUMO's popularity within the research on V2X or not, may be provable by evaluating the citations of following papers, trying to determine how often [25] is cited. This was not done so far.

As "V2X" covers about 70 % of the publications, its sub-topics may be investigated using the same approach. Figure 7 shows the development of sub-topics of "V2X" along the years. The overall frequencies of "V2X" sub-topics are as following:

- simulation packages: 28.6 %
- routing protocols: 26.5 %,
- applications: 22.4 %,

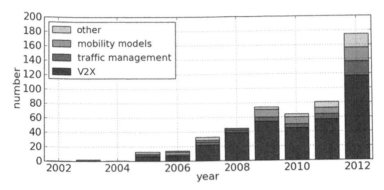

**Fig. 6.** Development of the publications' major topics. Top: absolute numbers, bottom: percentage, both along the years.

- PHY/MAC and mobility models: 5.1 % each,
- Other: 12.2 %.

It is interesting to note that "simulation packages" – presentation of tools for research – is dominant to such a high degree. On the other hand, one should take into regard that the presentation of a "simulation package" occurs often in combination with some further evaluation of V2X functionality, may it be a "routing protocol", or an "application", see also Fig. 5. Nonetheless, the author finds the number of reports on "simulation packages" quite high. Whether such "simulation packages" find their way into a broader use, or are only used once, and whether the necessity to develop new ones exist, given the high number of existing ones, is matter of a different kind of research.

A promising fact is the increase in using SUMO for evaluating V2X-based applications, as in most cases, such research requires a joint operation of a traffic simulation and a communication simulation, usually employing a middleware instance. The increase of publications on this topic shows that available middleware solutions are

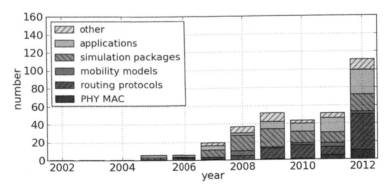

**Fig. 7.** Development of the publications' sub-topic within the "V2X" topic. Top: absolute numbers, bottom: percentage, both along the years.

accepted and can be used for scientific work. Within the work on "routing protocols", SUMO is usually used to generate vehicular "traces" only, which are then exported into a format readable by the used communication simulator.

The document sets of the remaining major topics are too small for a meaningful insight into the development over time. Figure 8 shows the distribution of the subtopics within the major topics "mobility models" and "traffic management". Further subdivisions are not represented due to the low number of documents that were assigned to them.

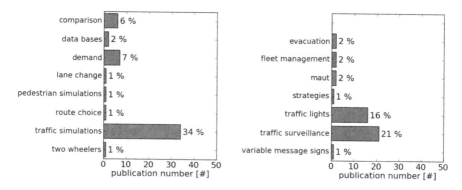

**Fig. 8.** Subtopics and their relative frequency for the topics "mobility models" (left) and "traffic management" (right).

## 5.6 Countries and Organizations

The categorization into the institutions the authors belong to is shown on the top-most, national level only, herein. Figure 9 shows a matrix of international co-authoring of the collection's papers, whereas Fig. 10 shows the numbers of publications per country.

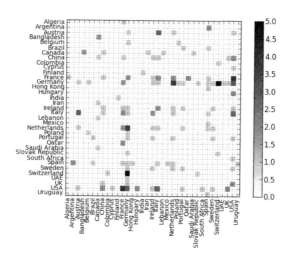

**Fig. 9.** Co-occurrence of countries within the collection.

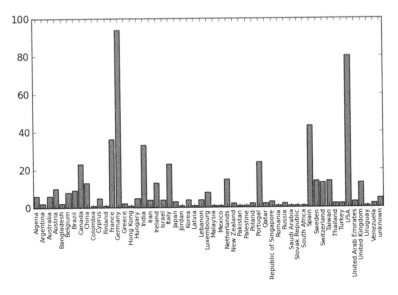

**Fig. 10.** The number of publications per country.

## 6  Summary

A collection of documents that name the traffic simulation SUMO was evaluated. The major interest was in determining whether SUMO got accepted by the scientific community, who uses it and how. For obtaining the presented results, the documents' bibliographic references as well as a manual classification performed on the documents were.

Different views on the collection were presented. The evaluations show the progress of using SUMO, the major topics it is applied for, and other aspects. Summarizing, it is possible to state that the number of publications increases and that no hints for a change in this development are visible. SUMO itself is accepted as a tool useful for research, indicated by the growing number of publications that report its usage. The researches which cite or use SUMO come from all over the world, albeit European countries and the USA dominate. Research on vehicular communication is the major application topic to be found within the papers and, if extrapolating the numbers, one should assume that it remains at this position for the next future.

The shown distributions and developments over time are a coarse look at the data set only. One could think of other evaluations and according visualization. In addition, further classification schemes could be used, such as features of the simulation, characteristics of used scenarios, the used references to SUMO and many more. Such extensions of the database may be performed in the future.

As one could assume, the collection itself is of a high value, pointing to already done, classified work, or to parties working on certain topics. Nonetheless, the work on the collection – collecting, scanning, reading, and classifying the documents – gave probably more insight and surprises than a view on the finished collections as presented here.

**Acknowledgements.** The author wants to thank all authors of the evaluated documents. The work would be not possible without free search engines and library portals mentioned earlier. Also, acknowledgements go to the developers of the open source tools used in this research, namely JabRef, Python, and matplotlib.

# References

1. Krajewicz, D., Erdmann, J., Behrisch, M., Bieker, L.: Recent development and applications of SUMO - Simulation of URBAN MObility. Int. J. Adv. Syst. Meas. **5**(3&4), 128–138 (2012)
2. DLR and contributors: SUMO homepage (2013). http://sumo.sourceforge.net/
3. Krajewicz, D.: Summary on publications citing SUMO, 2002–2012. In: Proceedings of the 1st SUMO Conference – SUMO 2013, pp. 11–24, DLR. ISSN: 1866-721X
4. Google: Google web search engine. http://www.google.com (2013). Accessed on 8 April 2013
5. Google: Google Scholar. http://scholar.google.com/ (2013). Accessed on 8 April 2013
6. BibTeX.org: http://www.bibtex.org/ (2013). Accessed on 8 April 2013
7. Wikipedia: BibTeX description. http://en.wikipedia.org/wiki/BibTeX (2013). Accessed on 8 April 2013
8. Google: Google Scholar alerts. http://googlesystem.blogspot.de/2010/05/email-alerts-for-google-scholar.html (2013). Accessed on 8 April 2013
9. Springer: Springer Link. http://link.springer.com (2013). Accessed on 8 April 2013
10. IEEE: IEEE Xplore. http://ieeexplore.ieee.org/ (2013). Accessed on 8 April 2013
11. ScienceDirect: ScienceDirect. http://www.sciencedirect.com/ (2013). Accessed on 8 April 2013
12. ACM: ACM Digital Library. http://dl.acm.org/ (2013). Accessed on 8 April 2013
13. Sommer, C., Dressler, F.: Progressing toward realistic mobility models in VANET simulations. Commun. Mag. IEEE **46**, 132–137 (2008)
14. Karnadi, F., Mo, Z., Lan, K.-C.: Rapid generation of realistic mobility models for VANET. In: Wireless Communications and Networking Conference, pp. 2506–2511 (2007)
15. Queck, T., Schünemann, B., Radusch, I., Meinel, C.: Realistic simulation of v2x communication scenarios. In: Proceedings of Asia-Pacific Services Computing Conference (APSCC 08), IEEE, pp. 1623–1627 (2008)
16. Rondinone, M., Maneros, J., Krajewicz, D., Bauza, R., Cataldi, P., Hrizi, F., Gozalvez, J., Kumar, V., Röckl, M., Lin, L., Lazaro, O., Leguay, J., Härri, J., Vaz, S., Lopez, Y., Sepulcre, M., Wetterwald, M., Blokpoel, R., Cartolano, F.: ITETRIS: a modular simulation platform for the large scale evaluation of cooperative ITS applications. Simul. Model. Pract. Theory (2013)
17. JabRef development team: JabRef web site. http://jabref.sourceforge.net/ (2013). Accessed on 8 April 2013
18. Python Software Foundation: Python Programming Language – Official Website. http://www.python.org/ (2013). Accessed on 8 April 2013
19. Hunter, J., Dale, D., Firing, E., Droettboom, M., The matplotlib development team: Matplotlib web site. http://matplotlib.org/ (2013). Accessed on 8 April 2013
20. Wikipedia: Stemming. http://en.wikipedia.org/wiki/Porter_stemmer (2013). Accessed on 8 April 2013
21. Porter, M.F.: An algorithm for suffix stripping. Program **14**(3), 130–137 (1980)
22. Feinberg, J.: Wordle™. http://www.wordle.net/ (2013). Accessed on 8 April 2013

23. Gupta, V., Yoo, D.: Python Porter stemming implementation. https://hkn.eecs.berkeley.edu/
    ~dyoo/python/py_lovins/ (2013). Accessed on 8 April 2013
24. Joerer, S., Sommer, C., Dressler, F.: Towards reproducibility and comparability of IVC
    simulation studies – A literature survey. Commun. Mag. **50**(10), 82–88 (2012). (IEEE, ISSN
    0163-6804)
25. Karnadi, F.; Mo, Z., Lan, K.-C.: MOVE: A MObility model generator for VEhicular
    network (2005)

# Author Index

Printed in the United States
By Bookmasters